Ashes to Awesome

JAPAN LIBRARY

Ashes to Awesome

YOSHIKAWA Hiroshi

Translated by Fred Uleman

Japan Publishing Industry Foundation for Culture

Japan's 6,000-Day Economic Miracle

Note to Readers: This book basically follows the Hepburn system of romanization. Family-name-first order for Japanese names has been retained. Macrons are used in people's and place names, except very common place names such as Tokyo.

Ashes to Awesome: Japan's 6,000-Day Economic Miracle
Yoshikawa Hiroshi. Translated by Fred Uleman.

Published by
Japan Publishing Industry Foundation for Culture (JPIC)
2-2-30 Kanda-Jinbocho, Chiyoda-ku, Tokyo 101-0051, Japan

First English edition: March 2021

© 1997, 2012 Yoshikawa Hiroshi
English translation © 2021 Japan Publishing Industry Foundation for Culture
All rights reserved

This book is a translation of *Kōdo seichō: Nihon o kaeta 6,000 nichi* (CHUOKORON-SHINSHA, INC., 2012), which was originally published by The Yomiuri Shimbun in 1997.
English publishing rights arranged with the author.

Jacket and cover design: Fukazawa Kōhei

Printed in Japan
ISBN 978-4-86658-175-0
https://japanlibrary.jpic.or.jp/

Contents

Preface to the English Edition

This is the English edition of my book *Kōdo seichō*, which was first published by The Yomiuri Shimbun in 1997. Happily, it was widely read and was later republished as a Chūkō Bunko paperback in 2012. Now the Japan Publishing Industry Foundation for Culture (JPIC) has kindly had it translated into English.

Japan's rapid growth during the 1950s and 1960s is doubtless a "once upon a time" story by now, and Japan has experienced many ups and downs since the rapid growth ended at the beginning of the 1970s. During the go-go years in the 1980s, some hailed Japan as number one. Once the bubbles burst at the beginning of the 1990s, however, Japan entered a long tunnel of economic stagnation. People talked about "the lost decade," and then about "the lost two decades" and even "the lost three decades." In the midst of all of this, the term "Japanization" was coined to mean contracting the economic malaise inflicted by the combination of slow growth and deflation.

That said, Japan deserves our attention both for having been the first non-Western country to succeed in transforming itself from a pre-modern society into a modern industrial state and for having rebuilt this modern industrial state from the ashes of defeat in World War II. Even today, many developing countries struggle to do what Japan did twice. While recognizing that economic growth is no longer regarded as the be all and end all goal and that sustainable growth is called for, we cannot ignore the fact that the average life expectancy remains forty years in some countries that have failed to modernize. In that context, I see Japan's postwar growth as an overall success story and hope it is of interest to many people outside of Japan.

In closing, I would like to thank Fred Uleman for his excellent translation and Nakaizumi Kiyoshi and Ozaki Izumi of JPIC for shepherding this project through to completion.

Yoshikawa Hiroshi
January 3, 2021

Introduction

Japan's economic miracle. It seems like so long ago. For the more than 40 percent of today's Japanese who were born after the miracle ended, talk of rapid growth seems like a fairy tale—a "once upon a time" story. Even for people who lived through those heady years, the memories have faded and the story has been relegated to history.

After the Korean War wound down with the armistice in 1953, there was a period of a decade and a half or so in which the Japanese economy achieved unprecedented growth averaging approximately 10 percent per annum. This rapid growth transformed not just the economy but every aspect of Japanese life. The changes were so sweeping that it is hard to remember what Japan was like before.

For an idea of the scope of these changes, let us first look at a few figures for the Japan of 1950, before the rapid growth had started. As of that year, 48 percent of the entire Japanese workforce was employed in the primary sector (farming, fishing, and forestry). In effect, nearly half of Japan's working population could be classified as agrarian. Only a third of female students went on to high school after completing their compulsory education (nine grades through junior high school). And half of the boys graduating from junior high went straight into the workforce. The exchange rate was 360 yen to the dollar and the per-capita national income was a scant 124 dollars—seven percent of the figure for the United States. The average life span (life expectancy at birth) was 58.0 years for men and 61.5 years for women.

A mere 20 years later, when the rapid-growth era ended in 1970, the percentage of the workforce engaged in the primary sector had fallen to 19 percent. Conversely, the "employed" proportion had grown to 64 percent. In just 20 years, almost two-thirds of the working population had come to be salaried workers. The percentage of junior-high graduates going on to high school had jumped to over 80 percent, and the ratios were about the same for both boys and girls. Per-capita national income was about 40 percent of the

US level, a stupendous increase from the 7 percent of two decades earlier. At the same time, life expectancy had jumped to 69.3 years for men and 74.7 years for women, putting Japan near the top of the world rankings.

Today, early in the second decade of the new century, Japan's society and economy have undergone even further changes—yet these changes pale by comparison with those that took place in the rapid-growth years. All of the things that we take for granted about our society and economy—all of the assumptions that define today's Japanese—were essentially structured and put in place during the rapid-growth years. Indeed, it is no exaggeration to say that the changes that took place then altered the very foundations of the Japanese nation.

Japanese history is conventionally broken down into periods, such as Heian (794–1185), Kamakura (1185–1333), and Edo (1603–1868), each with distinctive political, economic, and social characteristics. In that sense, the rapid-growth era fully deserves to be classified as a separate period by virtue of the impact it had and the changes it effected in our economic and social institutions. Unlike Japan's earlier historical periods, which generally spanned centuries, this one lasted less than two decades. The achievement of such a radical transformation in a mere 6,000 days is nothing less than astounding, and it deserves elucidation.

Looking back from today's perspective, the Japan of the early 1950s was a frightfully humble abode riddled with relics of the past. Were today's young people to be transported back to the Japan of that earlier age, they would probably see it all as a movie set and wonder where in the world the movie was supposed to be set. In any event, they would certainly see it as a poor country.

The rapid-growth years brought all kinds of material goods and vastly enriched our lives. Yet at the same time, there was much we lost in the process, and it is impossible to state with confidence that today's Japan is a socially richer and better place than it was before rapid growth transformed the nation. As the author and literary critic Yoshida Ken'ichi (1912–1977) commented,

> People talk about "the good old days," but that is a tricky notion. Every era has some good to it, and when the era passes, it is often the good alone that is remembered, which leads people to believe that the past was a better time. Of course, it is not that only the good disappears with

the era, but it is the good aspects that are missed. It is the good that lingers in our memories and causes people to talk about Tokyo today and the Tokyo of times past and to assert that yesteryear's Tokyo represented "the good old days" even though life in Tokyo is clearly better today. I suspect this goes beyond mere nostalgia, includes an appreciation of the culture that flourished in the Tokyo of yore, and conclude that today's Tokyo pales by comparison. From there, it is easy to indiscriminately come to the conclution that today's Tokyo has gone bad and that people who live there today live wretched lives in a wretched place. ("Tōkyō no machi" [Village Tokyo], *Seishun to Dokusho*, October 1974)

While it may be possible to rebut Yoshida's assertion that we have lost Tokyo as a cultural center, there is no refuting the fact that the years of extraordinary economic growth were also years of unprecedented environmental degradation. The extent of this degradation is clear for all to see. We have done irreparable damage to the natural world that has sustained us ever since the origin of our species. But is it fair to characterize this rapid growth as a Mephistophelian trap into which we fell? In this book, I look back at the rapid-growth years—which I characterize as a historical leap—in an effort to discern what they meant for all of us.

CHAPTER 1

Looking Back
Japan before Growth Took Off

Kimura Ihei's *Student Newlyweds*, 1949.

Postwar Chaos

History is always and inevitably a story of both continuities and discontinuities, so our effort to explain today's Japan could start anywhere—perhaps
with the Tokugawa shogunate (generally dated as 1603–1868), or perhaps
with the Meiji Restoration that ended the shogunate's rule. Japan's surrender
in August 1945 was another major turning point for the country. Indeed, the
consumer durables, population mobility, and other conspicuous markings of
Japan's rapid postwar economic growth were so transformational that it is
entirely reasonable to start more recently, with the democratization and other
systemic changes that followed the end of World War II and sparked a more
visible revolution. Japan's rapid growth was clearly born of defeat.

Of course, even though there were major legal and economic changes with
the start of the postwar Occupation, that does not mean there were immediate changes in the lives of ordinary people. As this chapter discusses, the
people's lives and the appearances of their communities were very strongly
tied to what might be called the prewar *ancien régime*. That said, the war
itself marked a major deterioration, pushing living standards and the like
well below prewar levels, and people had to basically start over from scratch
in many areas.

As of 1946, the year after the war ended, Japan's gross national product (GNP)
had fallen to half of its 1938 prewar peak. Not only had the vast majority of Japan's
factories and machinery been destroyed in the war, but the supply of imported raw
materials had been cut off. Steel production, for example, had fallen to an abysmal
7 percent of its prewar high. Living conditions were wretched. In terms of caloric
intake, the prewar daily average of 2,200 kcal per person had fallen to less than
1,500 kcal per person immediately after the war.

The first economic white paper, issued under the title "Report on the State

Table 1. Average urban boys' physique by elementary school grade, 1937–46

	Year	First grade	Second grade	Third grade	Fourth grade	Fifth grade	Sixth grade
Height (cm)	1937	110.3	116.4	120.3	125.5	130.5	134.7
	1946	107.0	111.9	116.9	121.0	125.6	129.9
Weight (kg)	1937	18.4	20.4	22.5	24.7	27.2	29.8
	1946	17.6	19.6	21.3	23.3	25.2	27.5

Source: Headquarters for Economic Stabilization, *Keizai jissō hōkokusho* (Report on the State of the Economy), 1947.

of the Economy" (*Keizai jissō hōkokusho*) in July 1947, had a table showing that elementary school children's height and weight had both regressed approximately one year's worth during the war.

It was against this background that the postwar reforms—the promulgation of the new Constitution, the agrarian land reforms, the dissolution of the financial and industrial conglomerates (zaibatsu), the labor law reforms, the dismantling of the patriarchal *ie* system, and more—were implemented. We can see how drastic these postwar reforms were if we look at the systems that preceded them. Here it is enough to cite the example of the old *ie* (lit. "house") system that governed family affairs. Under this system, the head of the household (generally the family patriarch) was the final arbiter in all family matters, with the authority to decide where household members lived and to approve or veto a prospective marriage partner for anyone in "his" household up to the age of 35. His wife was legally without standing, the same as the family's children. It is nearly impossible for us today to imagine a society largely based on a legal system giving the head of the household such absolute authority. Little wonder the vast bulk of the population welcomed the postwar reforms with the same sense of liberation that we feel on seeing a clear blue sky after weeks of overcast weather and rain.

Of course, these reforms were no panacea for the pressing issue of reviving the economy. The shot in the arm that the Japanese economy needed was provided by the Korean War–related special procurements starting in 1951, but even that boost left the economy about 15 percent below its prewar peak. The immediate postwar period of 1945–50 has often been termed an age of confusion, epitomized by the shortages of material goods and the plague of inflation run rampant. In a mere five years, consumer prices rose 70-fold. And this is just the figure derived from the official prices. In real life, things were far more expensive, if they were available at all, on the black markets that sprung up everywhere. In 1946–47, when the black markets flourished most conspicuously, it was estimated that their prices were anywhere from five to seven times the official prices set by the government.

This raging inflation had a major impact on society in a number of ways. In February 1946, for example, the Monetary Emergency Measures Ordinance was issued mandating that all money be deposited in banks and that people would be allowed to withdraw only the minimum needed to live on; anything beyond that was frozen in the bank. As a result of this ordinance, some 70 percent of all bank deposits were frozen and, with inflation, their value was eroded down to about one-fourth their initial value. Sorimachi Shigeo, a famous antique book dealer, reminisced about these times:

> It was truly tyrannical. Everybody, no exceptions, top to bottom, was forced to get by on a fixed monthly amount ranging from 500 yen (for a married couple with no children) to a maximum of 1,000 yen (couple with four children). This was everyone—even the imperial family, the aristocracy from dukes down to barons, and magnates like Mitsui Hachirōemon, Iwasaki Hisaya, and Sumitomo Kichizaemon—along with all the rest of us. By way of reference, the starting salary for a young policeman was 420 yen a month, and that for a new hire who had passed the higher civil service examination was 540 yen a month.
>
> You might call it lawless. You might call it tyrannical. But it happened, and there was nothing we could do about it in the post-surrender pandemonium. There would have been riots everywhere if the government had tried this in ordinary times, but the surrender had drained all of our fighting spirit and we had neither the energy nor the spirit to protest. Even if the people had protested, the full weight of the Occupation army would have been brought to bear to quash any dissent. Merchants like me were not even able to get the money we needed to pay for inventory. (*Ichi koshoshi no omoide* [Heibonsha, 1988], vol. 3)

Like savings, government bonds, corporate bonds, equity shares, and all the rest were rendered virtually worthless. Added to the agrarian land reform and the dissolution of the zaibatsu, the inflation and bank freeze were devastating for rich people. Sorimachi also quotes a number of affluent individuals lamenting the need to part with some rare books in February 1947: "It's because I have to pay that new wealth tax. But all my money's been

Table 2. Shares of incomes in national income (%)

	1934–36	1946	1947	1948	1949	1950
Wages	39.3	31.8	33.2	43.2	43.5	42.6
Self-employed	32.4	64.0	65.1	54.5	47.4	45.9
(Farming)	14.5	28.6	26.8	23.1	20.8	19.1
(Manufacturing)	3.8	8.8	11.8	10.2	9.5	12.2
(Commerce)	8.3	9.3	12.9	11.4	9.1	4.8
Rent	10.3	1.1	0.8	0.7	0.7	0.8
(Farmland rent)	4.4	0.3	0.2	0.1	0.1	0.1
Interest	6.9	2.0	0.9	0.8	1.1	1.4
Corporate earnings	8.3	1.0	1.0	2.4	5.1	9.1
Total	100.0	100.0	100.0	100.0	100.0	100.0

Source: Economic Deliberation Agency, *Sengo no kokumin shotoku* (Postwar National Income), 1953.

impounded and I don't have access to any of it. So I have no choice but to sell off some things." Thus did postwar society get its start with the fall of the old moneyed class.

There is one more striking change that this period engendered: Even as incomes plunged for urban salaried workers and incorporated firms, there was a sharp income uptick for sole proprietors operating as farmers, merchants, and manufacturers. In the midst of generalized deprivation so severe that elementary school children's height and weight were set back a full year, the people who dealt in tangibles emerged as winners. The farmers who grew rice, the sole proprietors who got their hands on this or that through all manner of underground routes, the merchants who sold some things at the government-mandated official prices but made their real money in the black market—these were the people whose situation stood in sharp contrast to the plight of the urban employees shown in Table 2.

This basic inequality persisted essentially unchanged until 1950. Indeed, it was not until the San Francisco Peace Treaty was signed in September 1951 and the Occupation was ended (except for Okinawa) in April 1952 that this immediate postwar chaos wound down. This is what Japan was like on the dawn of the rapid-growth years. Here let us take a closer look at how society was structured and how the people lived before the transformation got underway.

Village Life

As of 1950, fully half of Japan's workforce consisted of farmers. (More accurately, they were primary-sector workers—including those engaged in fishing and forestry—but here we call the primary sector "farming" and its workers "farmers" for simplicity's sake.) This is about the same percentage as in Indonesia today (in 2012). Elsewhere in 1950, the American agricultural sector accounted for only 12 percent of the US workforce, with the UK figure even lower at 5 percent. Among the industrialized countries, Italy was close to the Japanese figure at 46 percent. It is thus instructive to look at life in rural villages as representative of conditions in Japan, a semi-agricultural country at the time.

The big postwar upheaval in rural villages was caused by agrarian land reform. Pre-reform, 46 percent of the farmland had been worked by tenant farmers. In 1949, that figure was down to 13 percent. Paralleling this, the percentage of farmers who did not own any farmland at all fell from a prewar 28 percent to a postwar 8 percent as raging inflation made it essentially painless for tenant farmers to buy the land they farmed. Seen from the other side of the transaction, the landlords ended up effectively giving their land away. The combination of agrarian land reform and rampant inflation worked major changes in the land ownership and income patterns in rural villages. Along with this great leveling, these changes transformed the rural villages from scenes of frequent tenant uprisings protesting blatant inequalities into stable bastions of postwar conservatism.

Yet despite these major—indeed, revolutionary—reforms, rural life itself did not change all that much. Whether in micro terms or in macro terms, the postwar rural village was not much different from the prewar village. The number of farming households was surprisingly stable from the Meiji era (1868–1912) at roughly 5.5 million. In 1910, for example, it was 5.42 million; in 1938, 5.44 million. Accounting for this population stability was labor mobility. As Watanabe Shin'ichi, Nojiri Shigeo, Fukutake Tadashi, Honda Tatsuo, and other scholars pointed out even before the postwar reforms, the mechanism worked as follows.

The traditional model of a farm family was a couple with five children. Of the five, on average one would die in childhood. Of the remaining four, one boy (typically the eldest son) would stay on to take care of the farm when their parents died, two sons would find employment elsewhere, and the daughter would be married off. With the typical farm family sending two children to work elsewhere, and with the average "generation" of 30 years, that meant 12,000 people moving out every year. This outflow kept the number of farm households steady at around 5.5 million. This pattern of children moving from farm to city was temporarily interrupted by agrarian reform and other factors in the immediate postwar period, but it had basically reverted to form by 1950 or so and the number of farm households was again stable.

Looking at life in rural Japan reveals even more striking continuity. The village—and this is not the village as an administrative unit but rather the village as it formed naturally during the Edo period (1603–1868) or earlier as people came together in geographical proximity and formed communities—typically consisted of 50–60 farming households, each living in a thatched-roof farmhouse in the middle of the family's fields. The houses, family life, and village life were very much as described by Kon Wajirō in his *Nihon no minka* (Japanese Rural Homes), published by Suzuki Shoten in 1922 and later republished by Iwanami Shoten in 1989. In addition to a dirt-floor foyer (*doma*) connecting the outside work area and the inside work/living space, there was a large wooden-floored area divided into a number of rooms. Of these, it was the *chanoma* adjacent to the *doma* that was the center of family life. As Kon describes it:

> The *chanoma* floor is typically bare wood where people sit on thin rush mats. The *irori* [sunken hearth] is always in this room, and the family sits around it to work and to eat. There is an established etiquette on where the head of the household, his wife, guests, and help sit, typically as shown in the illustration [Figure 1]. The place of honor facing the *doma* and entrance is called the *yokoza* and is reserved for the head of the household. His wife and family sit to his left, nearest the kitchen, in what is called, when it is named at all, the *kakaza*. Guests are to his right, farthest from the kitchen and facing the wife and family, in the *kyakuza*. The help sit facing the head of the household with their backs to the *doma*. Because this is where the butt of the firewood protruded, it is called the *kinojiri* [wood butt]. These people are also responsible for tending the fire. The actual names given to these places vary from one part of the country to another, but the who-sits-where rules are the same everywhere.

When the man of the house got old and turned the household over to his son, the son, from that day on, sat in the *yokoza*. This tradition was preserved

Figure 1. The traditional Japanese farmhouse

Typical layout patterns

Nasu Ginzō house in Hyūga-Shiibason,
Miyazaki Prefecture
Source: Kon Wajirō, *Nihon no minka*
(Japanese Rural Homes).

Storage	Kitchen	*Doma*
Guest room	*Cha-noma*	

Pattern 1

Guest room	Kitchen	*Doma*
Misc. room	*Cha-noma*	

Pattern 2

Guest room	Storage	Kitchen	*Doma*
Misc. room 2	Misc. room 1	*Cha-noma*	

Pattern 3

Seating around the *irori*

	Father	
Guests	*Irori*	Family
	Help	

Doma

Family sitting around the *irori*. (Photo by Nakamata Masayoshi)

in the rural homes, or *minka*, that Kon described, and this generalized set of assumptions formed the basis for the *ie* system under the prewar Civil Code. It was assumed this *minka* would be home to the grandparents, young parents, and their children.

Next to the *chanoma* was the kitchen. Everything there had been passed down from generation to generation. Because there was no running water, there was rudimentary plumbing to bring in water from the well. And in lieu of gas, wood and charcoal were the primary fuels for the cooking hearth and stove. There would also be an iron pot for cooking, a metal rack for grilling fish, and an alumite kettle. Aside from these items, just about all of the utensils were made of wood or bamboo.

Turning to the *doma*, one would have seen traditional footwear, such as wooden *geta* and straw sandals. Hanging from the ceiling was an unshaded light bulb to provide illumination. There was, of course, no washing machine. Instead, there was a washboard used to scrub the laundry with soap; rinsing might be done in a nearby creek (as in the famous opening passage of the tale of Momotarō [Peach Boy], where the old man goes off to collect wood and the old woman goes down to the creek to do the wash), and the clothes hung out to dry.

All of the farm work was muscle-powered. Agricultural machinery was not yet available, so the main tools were the shovel, the hoe, and a cart that was pulled by hand. Half of the families had a cow and about one in five had a horse they could use to do the plowing. Typically, every garden had free-roaming chickens everywhere.

This picture of rural life, unimaginable today, endured until at least 1950. Not only was it not mechanized, the village was basically able to survive on its own. Families made their own footwear as well as their own dried fruit, miso, soba, and mochi, did their own mending, stuffed their own futon—the list goes on. And for jobs requiring many hands, such as rethatching farmhouse roofs, villagers would work as a team using traditional skills handed down over the generations.

While it is virtually impossible to find precise data quantifying how self-sufficient the rural community was in economic terms, Table 3 provides some indicative numbers from a 1950 survey of farm households conducted by the Ministry of Agriculture and Forestry.

Excepting Hokkaido, where farms were conspicuously larger, average annual farm earnings were about 110,000 yen, a figure derived by adding the cash earnings from farming (70,000 yen) and the cash earnings from forestry and other activities (60,000 yen) and subtracting tax payments (20,000 yen).

On the consumption side of the ledger, farm families had some things they purchased and some things they made for themselves or acquired outside the cash economy. The survey attempted to estimate the cash value of the latter. As shown in Table 3, some 90 percent of their rice, wheat, and other staple foods were self-sourced. Looking at foodstuffs overall, including edible oils, sake, and tobacco, the breakdown between items that were purchased and those that were not was 28,000 to 63,000 yen, meaning that they were self-sufficient for about 70 percent of their foodstuffs. For consumption overall, the breakdown was 90,000 to 72,000 yen, indicating a self-sufficiency ratio of about 44 percent.

Of the things in which they were conspicuously self-sufficient, firewood and charcoal (1,720 to 6,992) stand out. This is particularly striking in comparison with electricity (1,714 to 1). Including electricity, they were self-sufficient for about two-thirds of their utilities. Overall, farm households were essentially half self-sufficient even at this point after the war. This changed dramatically during the period of rapid growth. In 1970, as the rapid-growth period drew to an end, farm households were only about one-third self-sufficient in food and only 11 percent self-sufficient in total consumption.

By way of reference, the share of spending on foodstuffs relative to total spending (Engel's coefficient) was 0.56 in 1950—very close to the Chinese figure of 0.54 in 1990. However, it then declined as incomes increased to stand at 0.32 in 1970 and 0.23 in 1995.

This was Japan in 1950—where farming families maintained many of the old traditions in the nooks and crannies of their lives, where their communities were about half self-sufficient, and where they accounted for about half of the working population—or well over half if minors and seniors are included.

Urban Life

What was urban life like around this time? It was certainly quite different from rural life. In 1951, for example, an Henri Matisse exhibition drew 150,000 visitors to the Tokyo National Museum over a 44-day period. The future was stirring in the city.

Even so, there was not much difference between urban and rural in terms of material poverty. If anything, it was the urban employed who bore the brunt of the chaos in the immediate aftermath of the war. While there were some people who made a killing in the black market or other pursuits and

Table 3. Farm household budgets, 1950 average (excluding Hokkaido)

			Purchased (yen)	Not purchased (value in yen)
Food and beverages	Foodstuffs	Rice	3,403	37,028
		Wheat	1,169	7,608
		Other grains	25	449
		Potatoes	52	2,460
		Legumes	100	1,080
		Vegetables	338	7,138
		Seaweed, wet and dried	527	118
		Fish and shellfish	5,467	134
		Meat, eggs, and dairy products	1,048	1,682
		Processed foods	1,110	60
	Seasonings and oils		4,460	4,600
	Consumed for pleasure	Alcoholic beverages	2,898	97
		Tobacco	4,217	2
		Sweets, fruit, and beverages	2,868	947
	Communal dining, eating out, and school lunches		292	3
Total			27,974	63,406
Clothing	Clothing		14,800	111
	Footwear and protective gear		3,131	26
Utilities	Electricity		1,714	1
	Charcoal		1,720	6,992
	Other utilities		248	4
Housing	Rent, repairs, and depreciation		3,616	37
	Furniture and fixtures		6,584	2
Healthcare	Services		2,135	1
	Goods		4,234	1
Transportation and communication	Transportation		1,939	–
	Communications		273	0
School and educational expenses			3,576	1
Amusement and entertainment			3,218	4
Socializing	Gifts		4,970	1,278
	Entertaining people at home		1,206	61
Miscellany and depreciation			3,944	17
One-off expenses (e.g., marriages, celebrations, and funerals)			5,034	409
Total			90,316	72,351

Source: Ministry of Agriculture and Forestry, *Nōka keizai chōsa hōkoku* (Survey of Farm Household Economy).

suddenly got rich, such people were a decided minority. When only a third of the population nationwide could be counted as employed and drawing a salary, the figure for Tokyo was 70 percent. It was these salaried employees and their families who suffered the most abject poverty in the tumultuous postwar years. Unlike rural farm families, they were completely dependent upon the government rationing system and were hard-pressed to find enough to eat.

It was not until 1950 that glimmerings of stability returned to these people's lives. That was the year government controls and rationing were abolished for food and clothing. With the winding down of the horrendous inflation and all of the difficulties and confusion it had caused, the currency was redesigned and a new 1,000 yen bill was issued, with Prince Shōtoku featured as the "face" of Japanese money. The next year, a series of commemorative stamps was issued showing the top 100 tourist destinations based on a newspaper poll asking readers to nominate their favorite spots. This was an impressive series of 20 sets of commemorative stamps, starting with the Zaō ski resort and featuring Nihondaira, Hakone, Ujigawa, Nagasaki, Shōsenkyō, and more before ending with Kintaikyō. The very idea that tourist spots could be featured on postage stamps would have been unimaginable just a few years earlier, and 1950–51 marked a return to normalcy for many people. What was urban life like at the time?

To begin with, urban life did not have the same potential for self-sufficiency that rural life had. Unlike farmers who could walk to their fields, urban employees lived much farther from their jobs and used the transportation infrastructure to get to work, much the same as they do today. Japanese cities had already begun to modernize in the 1920s, albeit to a rather limited extent. The Dōjunkai apartment buildings in Omotesandō and Daikan'yama—the first of which was torn down in 1996—were originally built in the 1920s and were relics of that era's modernization. Likewise the office buildings in Marunouchi and the department stores in Nihonbashi—impressive structures that speak eloquently of that earlier era's achievements in modernization. With much of that heritage remaining, Japanese cities in the 1950s were definitely on track to becoming today's metropolises. However, we are not here to dwell on the continuities. Rather, it is the discontinuities that are arresting. Shibuya's Hachikō square, adjacent to the world-famous scramble crossing, for example, looks very different in the early postwar photo overleaf than it does today.

The differences are even more striking if we look at the lives of Japan's urban denizens then and now. First is housing. Tokyo, Osaka, Hiroshima,

Nagasaki, and other major urban centers all had numerous neighborhoods that had been reduced to rubble by the intensive bombing and fires during the war. As a result, all of these cities experienced severe housing shortages. In Tokyo, for example, some 310,000 people—about 10 percent of the postwar population—were living in makeshift shelters. There was no glass in the windows. Instead, heavy oiled paper was put up over the openings in these hovels. This housing shortage was then exacerbated by the 500,000 to 600,000 people who moved into the metropolis every year, including people returning from Japan's former overseas possessions. People were reduced to relying on relatives, former neighbors, or anyone else they might know for a place to live. It was rare for just one family to occupy a home, and there were parts of Tokyo where three families to a home was the norm.

Despite this, new home construction proceeded at a snail's pace. Before and during the war, about 70 percent of the urban population lived in rented quarters. Even such luminaries as Mori Ōgai and Natsume Sōseki rented. Rents went up, there was fierce inflation, and the tax rates on both land and residences jumped from the prewar 3 percent to a postwar 40 percent. Within this, the inflation was far greater in construction costs (about 200 times prewar levels) than in rents (about 50 times prewar levels), and people quickly figured out that there was no money to be made in building and renting residences. As the prewar landlords were reduced to poverty, the development of new housing in the urban areas was nil. While the first glimmerings of stability and a little leeway were showing up in urban life by 1950, shortly before the rapid growth took off, the urban housing situation was little changed from what it had been during the immediate postwar chaos. This scramble for housing stood in sharp contrast to the situation in rural areas, where farmers still had their thatched-roof houses from earlier times.

Even when urban residents were able to find housing, the situation inside was dismaying at best. Photos such as Kimura Ihei's 1949 *Gakusei kekkon* (Student Newlyweds) at the start of this chapter show how spartan living conditions were. It is worth spending some time looking at what these young people had by way of household possessions. First was an iron rice pot on a small charcoal stove made of clay, called a *shichirin*. This *shichirin* was apparently named for being so small and efficient that you could cook a whole meal on just seven (*shichi*) *rin* worth of charcoal, about 7/1,000 of one yen. Beside it was a wooden container to hold the rice once it was cooked. Both the rice pot and the container were new—part of the bride's dowry. The room

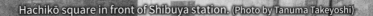
Hachikō square in front of Shibuya station. (Photo by Tanuma Takeyoshi)

would be the size of about 4.5 tatami mats, roughly 7.4 square meters. Inside, the young master of the house sits reading his newspaper, in front of him a rectangular *hibachi* with a cooking pot and a tea kettle on it. Behind him is a chest for china and other table settings. Both the *shichirin* and the *hibachi* burn charcoal. Running water is available in the communal kitchen.

These are young people, but they are not particularly impoverished. At the time, urban households did not typically have washing machines, refrigerators, television sets, or telephones. The light, such as it was, was a single unshaded bulb dangling from the ceiling. Unlike the rural areas, cities had running water by this point. In Tokyo's case, this was supplied from a large filtration plant and water works in Nishi-Shinjuku—the area west of Shinjuku Station that is now home to the Tokyo Metropolitan Government offices and a number of hotels and high-rise office buildings. Still, aside from the diffusion rates for running water and the availability of gas for heating and cooking, there were no substantial differences between the home appliances and furnishings that urban and rural households owned. Of course, there were minor differences, such as the rural household's owning an iron pot and the urban household's owning an aluminum one, but both urban and rural were bereft of all the appliances, conveniences, and other amenities that we take for granted in the modern home.

In fact, city life was still largely a continuation of earlier traditions, albeit not as much as rural life was. Take mosquito netting, for example. This was an essential summer item for every family, even though it largely disappeared from people's lives when window screens and the like were introduced during the rapid-growth era, essentially making the entire house a giant mosquito net and eliminating the need for netting in any particular room.

Natsume Sōseki's *Kōjin* (serialized in 1912–13; translated by Beongcheon Yu as *The Wayfarer* [Detroit: Wayne State University Press, 1967]) includes the passage: "As I lay with my head near the window I could see the sky through the net. I tucked up the red hem of the net and put just my head out. The stars were glittering in the sky." When Iwanami Shoten republished this in *Sōseki zenshū* (The Complete Works of Natsume Sōseki) in 1966, they added a footnote explaining that this "red hem" is the hem of the mosquito netting, which was made of red cloth. This strikes someone like me, who slept under mosquito netting every summer, as wildly unnecessary, since we can immediately picture the nets' red hems. Yet for someone too young to have ever used mosquito netting, it is probably woefully inadequate and does nothing to conjure up the image evoked. While perhaps a minor example, this shows how Japanese in the 1950s, like myself, shared a typical everyday experience with Sōseki.

We can actually go back much farther than that. Suzuki Harunobu (ca. 1725–1770), who is credited with having invented the *nishiki-e* style of woodblock prints, included mosquito netting in a number of his prints. So at least as far as mosquito netting goes, Japanese life in the 1950s was not much different from what it had been in the eighteenth century.

Similar examples are easy to find. Irokawa Daikichi notes, for instance, in his 1990 *Shōwa-shi sesōhen* (A History

Suzuki Harunobu's depiction of the family mosquito net. (© Keiō Gijuku)

of Shōwa Social Life) that 82.4 percent of the children born in 1955 were delivered at home but this figure had dropped to a mere 1.2 percent by 1975. Home births were common not only in rural areas but nationwide. Even in Tokyo, 78 percent of all births were home births as late as 1950. This idea of giving birth at home with a midwife's help goes back not to the Edo period but to much earlier times in Japanese history. Yet these ancient traditions and lifestyles were altered and extinguished one by one in the rapid-growth years.

Movies were the prime amusement for people in the 1950s. After all, people did not have televisions, and radio is a purely auditory experience, so it should be no surprise that big-screen movies in full color were quite an attraction. *Gone with the Wind* opened in September 1951 and was seen by 285,000 people in Tokyo alone. *Shane*, *Roman Holiday*, *East of Eden*, *Jeux interdits* (*Forbidden Games*), and many other blockbusters were all released in the early 1950s. Nor were they all foreign films. This was also a golden age for Japanese cinema, with outstanding films by such great directors as Ozu Yasujirō, Kurosawa Akira, and Mizoguchi Kenji.

Adults were not the only ones who were hungry for visual entertainment. For the children, there were *kami-shibai*, "paper plays" with a storyteller telling a story while showing illustrations. These were the most popular amusement and social space for children at the time. Essentially, the *kami-shibai* business

Children listen to a *kami-shibai* storyteller, ca. 1957. (© Kyodo News)

model involved going from neighborhood to neighborhood, attracting a group of children, and selling them sweets that they could enjoy along with the performance. At their peak, it is said there were 50,000 of these itinerant storytellers nationwide. Since the under-16 population at the time was about 30 million, that works out to one storyteller for every 600 children. And since Japan's labor force was 35 million, the storytellers would have accounted for one in every 700 working persons. Yet this art was destined to die out after rapid growth was underway and more and more families bought television sets.

Kami-shibai were not the only amusement the kids had. They also had *menko* (card flipping), *rōseki* (chalking graffiti in the streets), jump rope, and many other games that could be played out in the street or in a vacant lot. Even in the big cities, there were surprisingly many vacant lots and lanes free of vehicular traffic. These were ideal for children's games, many of which could be played with no toys or anything at all, like leapfrog.

Lest we forget, there were also rental bookstores where you could borrow the latest books very cheaply. The manga books at the time—such as *Shōnen*, *Shōjo*, and *Shōnen Gahō*—were monthlies, not weeklies. Tezuka Osamu's *Tetsuwan Atomu* (*Astro Boy*) started serializing in *Shōnen* in 1952. Children everywhere always look forward to reading the popular manga, but this was especially so in the early postwar period when such books were hard to come by. These rental bookstores were an ingenious solution in this time of scarcity.

Children had basically everything they needed right in the neighborhood, but that was not the case for adults. Unlike the people in rural villages, urban dwellers had to use the transportation infrastructure to go to work, to go to a department store, to go see a movie, and to do a lot of other things. For most, "the transportation infrastructure" meant streetcars. Of course, Tokyo also had the Yamanote Line running in a loop within the capital and the subway, although the Ginza Line between Shibuya and Asakusa was the only line operating at the time—this 14.3 kilometers a stark contrast to today's 13 lines totaling 304.1 kilometers. Some cities still have streetcars, but these are now seen as historic relics, ringing their bells as they trundle along. But being slow was not a problem then, since life was slower paced and nobody complained about how long it seemed to take to get from one place to another. Things were even slower in the winter, as few cities had snow removal for their streets, and even big cities like Sapporo relied upon horse-drawn sleighs to move things around in the winter. This—horse-drawn sleighs—is a scene that you will not see in any of the big cities now.

Not only were the cities slow, they were also poorly illuminated. There were not many streetlights, and it was very dark at night even in Tokyo outside of Ginza and a few other special areas. Looking again at the photo of the area just outside Shibuya Station around 1950, for example, it is clear that all of the billboards and other advertising was painted. There was no neon. True, there were streetlights here and there, and there was some light from the shops that were still open, but this was pretty much limited to the shopping and entertainment districts. The narrow streets elsewhere were basically unlit.

At best, there might be a single bare bulb and fixture attached to a wooden utility pole.

Tanizaki Jun'ichirō wrote about this in his *Ren'ai oyobi shikijō* (Love and Lust), serialized in *Fujin Kōron* in April–June 1931.

> City folk of today, in all probability, know nothing of true darkness. Or maybe it is not only city folk: since ours is a world in which of late street-lamps adorn even fairly isolated country neighborhoods, dark's dominion has gradually been driven away, and people finally have all forgotten what the darkness of night is. As I walked in the darkness of Beijing at that time, I thought, "This truly is night, how long have I forgotten the darkness of night." Then I felt a strange sense of nostalgia, recalling how chill and lonely, how terrible and wretched, were the nights when, as a child, I slept under the wavering light of a paper lantern. (As translated by Thomas LaMarre in *Shadows on the Screen* [University of Michigan Press, 2005].)

This is, of course, the same Tanizaki who wrote *In'ei Raisan* (*In Praise of Shadows*) and who had a special sensitivity to shadows and darkness. As Tanizaki tells it, Tokyo had already lost its "real night" by the 1920s. Yet even if we take Tanizaki's word for this, there was still a lot of murky darkness in Japan just prior to the start of the rapid-growth years, and the murky-dark nights disappeared only with rapid growth. People such as Tanizaki, who loved shadows and took shadow to be the essence of Japanese culture, likely believed that the loss of this nighttime darkness marked an existential transformation in the Japanese soul.

Whether rural or urban, people followed the old traditions in nearly every aspect of their lives right up to the rapid-growth years. The things they had and used were largely the same things that people had been using for countless generations. Conversely, they had very few of the everyday things that we take for granted today. Yet in just a few short years, the Japanese economy would embark upon a transitional super-express called rapid growth. It would be a ride of about a decade and a half that would largely reshape Japan's society and structure Japanese life as we know it today.

① My mom and dad really had a tough time scraping the money together for this sewing machine.
② I'm so unbelievably happy.
  Ho, ho, ho.
③ You have no idea how much I've wanted a sewing machine.
④ Now that I have this, I can make and mend the kids' clothes.

Tsuge Yoshiharu, "Mishin ga kita hi," in *Tsuge Yoshiharu zenshū* (Chikuma Shobō, 1993), vol.7.

What was it that the Japanese were so anxious to attain? What was it that fueled this high-speed rapid-growth ride? The answer was no secret. We were frantic to catch up with the amenities and lifestyle enjoyed by the industrialized Western nations, especially the United States.

The immediate postwar years were very much a hand-to-mouth, dog-eat-dog situation, and it was not until the early 1950s that things settled down a bit and people had the leeway to think about the American standard of living. In comparison to the destitution that characterized Japanese life during and right after the war, American life came across as a glittering grail to be pursued. America had enjoyed its rapid-growth era well ahead of Japan (in the 1920s) and was already a motorized society. America in the 1950s was the world's first mass-consumption society, and the Americans who came to Japan with the Occupation army brought the American way of life with them. The NHK radio program "Letter from America" (*Amerika-dayori*) described and exclaimed over this American way of life in great detail for its listeners. There was, for example, abundant information on American kitchen appliances: "You just put the bread in, push the lever, and a little while later, ding!—up pops a crispy brown slice of toast." Most Japanese hearing these descriptions could not believe such convenience existed. "Incredible" was the common reaction. A family car, home appliances, and more: all of these things were still very much out of reach for the average Japanese—things to dream of and ardently long for—and this longing also made them goals to be pursued and prizes to be won.

The Japanese consumer revolution started with clothing. Once women were free to change out of their *monpe*, the dowdy pantaloons that had been their wartime uniform, everyone wanted to learn how to sew Western clothing. Accompanying this, the treadle sewing machine became the first piece of modern machinery to find a place in the ordinary Japanese home. Every year, the post office issues numbered New Year postcards with a mid-January drawing for prizes. There is always a range of prizes, but in 1950 the *grand prix* was a sewing machine and first prize was clothing fabric. So great was the thrill of finally owning a sewing machine that Tsuge Yoshiharu worked it into one of his manga.

Another revolution that characterized this era was the invention of nylon. Tōyō Rayon (now Toray) had already expanded its nylon production facilities in 1949, but the company then spent an enormous sum of money (about 1.5 times its total capitalization) to license nylon technology from DuPont and to put the new nylon production technology online in 1951. Nylon's availability had a major impact not just on women's stockings, underwear, and other apparel but on a wide range of other manufactured items as well. For one specific example, nylon came to be used instead of swine hair for toothbrush bristles. Having anticipated latent consumer needs and established a strong position in nylon, Tōyō Rayon quickly caught up with Teijin, which had been the leading textile company during the war, and demonstrated the importance of new technology for all to see.

Starting with clothing, fluorescent lighting, and other "little" things for the home, the consumer revolution soon moved to more substantial durable goods. Particularly prominent here were washing machines, refrigerators, and television sets—jocularly labeled *sanshu no jingi*, the "three sacred treasures" of the modern home. These appliances are essential players in the rapid growth story.

Washing Machines

The first of the trio was the washing machine. The first washing machines went on sale in 1949 and were priced at 54,000 yen. This was about as much as the annual starting salary for a new university graduate going into the civil service and more than a third of the 140,000 yen average annual income for an urban working family at the time. Unsurprisingly, there were only about a score of them sold per month.

By 1953, however, the price had come down to less than 30,000 yen while the average annual income for an urban working family had gone up to 310,000 yen. With prices halved and incomes doubled, washing machines were four times more affordable. By 1955, washing machines were only about 20,000 yen and urban incomes were 360,000 yen. Sales reflected the change. In 1949, washing machine sales were only about 20 a month. Just six years later, in 1955, one in three households had a washing machine. They were obviously very enthusiastically welcomed, and the Akutagawa Prize–winning author Shigekane Yoshiko reflected on the sheer thrill of getting one of these treasures:

> I will never forget how excited I was when we got an electric washing machine. It was the biggest thrill of my life. Young people may well be tired of hearing this—what they think of as just another old woman's tale about the way things used to be—but I still feel a shiver of excitement even now when I think about it. The menfolk might talk about the Meiji Restoration (of the mid-nineteenth century) and how it changed things so much, but for us womenfolk it was the availability of these new appliances that revolutionized our lives.
>
> I was still in my twenties and doing the laundry by hand with all my might on a rough corrugated washboard. I have no idea when our forebears moved from stones by the river to washboards, but it probably goes back many centuries. I hear it is common worldwide for people to do their wash by laying it out on stones, stomping it, and then flailing it against the same stones, but these washboards were very much a Japanese woman's thing.
>
> So I was out there washing the diapers, the sheets, the men's white shirts, bedding covers, and everything else with this time-honored washboard for three or four hours every day. . . .
>
> And then we got a washing machine. We bought it on the installment plan, and it was so exciting to finally have it that I just stood there open-mouthed. I don't remember how long I spent just gazing in wonder as the spindle jerked this way and that doing my laundry for me. It was a fantastic sight, and I unconsciously put my hands together and said a silent prayer—both thanking the gods for this wondrous device and imploring them to please not punish me for this outlandish extravagance as I pinched myself and jumped for joy.
>
> The wringer was hand-cranked rollers, and I thought whoever came up with the idea of doing it this way was a genius and deserved a Nobel Prize. Even big things like sheets and bedding covers—things that I had had to wring with all my might—went through the rollers with no trouble. No wonder I was so awestruck by the ingenuity of it and wanted to make some votive offering to the rollers. (Shigekane Yoshiko, *Nyōbō no yuriisu* [Kōdansha, 1984])

In this excerpt, Shigekane was speaking for most Japanese women. When the diffusion rate reached one-third of households in 1955, the washing machine was added to the basket of goods used to calculate the consumer price index (CPI). The CPI is used to measure how the average price for a basket of consumer goods and services changes over time and is seen as a key economic indicator. This basket of goods and services is reviewed and revised every five years as new goods and services become available and consumer behavior patterns change. It included 580 items in 1996. Among the other things added along with the washing machine in 1955 were whale meat, sausage, Ajinomoto's MSG, Thermos bottles, radios, fluorescent lights, electric irons, suitcases, shampoo, bicycles, taxi fare, and having your hair permed. These were all cutting-edge goods and services at the time. Conversely, a number of things were dropped from the list in 1955, among them portable cooking stoves, kindling, and men's *tabi* (traditional ankle socks).

Television

Close on the washing machine's heels was television—whose arrival was, if anything, an even more exciting development for the average Japanese family.

The first television transmission was made on February 1, 1953, by national broadcaster NHK in Tokyo. That August, NHK was joined by Nippon Television, a private-sector broadcaster. But almost no households had television sets at this point. After all, a set cost 190,000 yen, which was more than 60 percent of the average working household's annual income of 310,000 yen. Using the same ratio and adjusting for current working-household income, it would be as if today's television sets were priced at 4 million yen. This was definitely not something most people could afford. The year NHK started television broadcasting, the number of households subscribed to the new service was a mere 866 in all of Japan. Diffusion was slow, the same as it had been for washing machines, and this was obviously a problem going forward for the broadcasters. Looking ahead, Nippon Television set up television sets for public viewing in the plazas outside Shinbashi, Shibuya, and other major train stations when it started broadcasting.

Given how important the sense of sight is, our thirst for and appreciation of the visual is visceral. Seeking to satisfy this appetite, we have gone in a steady linear progression from hand-drawn pictures on cave walls to photographs in albums and then to moving pictures on a screen. Even in the chaotic postwar years, movies were among the foremost forms of entertainment in the land, and box office ticket sales topped 700 million tickets on average every year. Television can be seen as an extension of the movies, but with added attractions: While the content of movies is basically limited to drama and other stories, television is able to broadcast sporting events live, to offer variety shows and musical programs, and to do so across a broader range of genres. Indeed, this distinction between movies and television holds even today, the very visible presence of movie-like television programs notwithstanding.

Among the most popular programs on television were sporting events and musical programs. There was, for example, professional wrestling featuring such superstars as Rikidōzan and professional baseball with teams such as the Nishitetsu Lions. Television broadcast these events far and wide, both enhancing the events' popularity and using them to boost and sustain television's own popularity. The same year the television stations started up, for example, they were able to broadcast a boxing match in which the Japanese boxer Shirai Yoshio, who had won the world flyweight title the previous year, successfully defended his title against challenger Terry Allen.

Rikidōzan and his karate chop were inordinately famous—so much so that I doubt there was anyone alive in Japan at the time who did not know his name. His matches followed a standard script: His dastardly opponent would commit all manner of foul deeds and Rikidōzan would end up bloodied but not beaten. Then, at the last minute, when all seemed lost, he would explode in a fury of karate chops, leaving his opponent (almost invariably an American) dazed and begging for mercy. This was a wildly popular act, very likely because it appealed to the Japanese resentment at having lost the war and to the desire to wreak vengeance on those who had humiliated Japan. Yet the psychology aside, this was spectacular entertainment quite different from the stories the movies told.

Professional baseball was also immensely popular in the 1950s, and among the players, none was more popular than the Nishitetsu Lions' pitcher Inao "Iron-Arm" Kazuhisa and batter Nakanishi Futoshi. For three years running starting in 1956, Nishitetsu faced the Yomiuri Giants in the Japan Series, winning all three years. There have been many baseball stars in subsequent years, but none to equal Inao, who was immortalized in the 1959 film *Tetsuwan tōshu: Inao monogatari* (The Iron-Arm Inao Story).

Although television sets were first installed outdoors for public viewing, and then in restaurants for diners to watch, television spread quickly to the

A crowd turns out to watch the televised finals of the All-Japan Professional Wrestling Championship match between Rikidōzan and Kimura Masahiko. (© Kyodo News)

home in the late 1950s. In addition to the many sports broadcasts, television got a major boost in 1958 when Shōda Michiko, the daughter of Nisshin Seifun President Shōda Hidesaburō, got engaged to marry Crown Prince Akihito. This engagement sparked what was called a Michi Boom, which had non-sports fans also glued to their television sets. The wedding was billed as the celebration of the century, and people rushed to buy television sets so they could watch it. As noted above, NHK had only 866 paying subscribers in 1953, the year broadcasting started, but in April 1959, when the wedding was held, that number topped 2 million. Symbolizing the arrival of the television age, Tokyo Tower was completed in 1958 as a broadcast tower.

The main reason television spread so quickly, though, was that incomes went up and television prices plunged. This was the same dynamic as had been seen with washing machines: they suddenly became affordable. Yet that was not the whole story, as it was the sports broadcasts, the royal wedding, and drama that movies could not match that made people want to buy television sets once they could afford them. Even today, television continues to provide unmatched drama and excitement for viewers of all ages, excitement of the sort that used to be available only on festival days. As Yanagita Kunio might well have observed, we were not supposed to talk during meals; everyone ate in silence. Anyone who was a child in the 1950s or earlier will be familiar with this injunction. Not only mealtime but most of the day was spent in silent concentration on the job at hand. Whether television really was the instrument of what Ōya Sōichi called "the idiotization of the population" or not, it definitely changed the rhythm of Japanese life by providing a constant stream of excitement and stimulus.

Television's unmatched popularity is graphed in Figure 2, which shows the different income strata's ownership ratios for the major consumer durables in 1966. Obviously, the more affluent cohorts owned more consumer durables and the less well-off families owned fewer. But even among the less well off, television ownership was far more common than ownership of other consumer durables. Almost all households with annual incomes of 300,000 yen

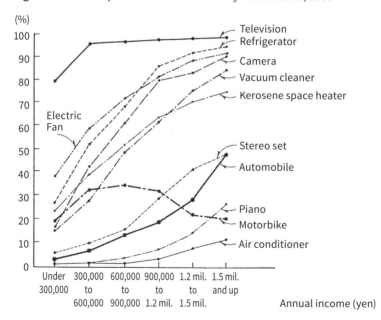

Figure 2. Ownership of consumer durables by income level, 1966

Source: Economic Planning Agency, Trends of Consumption and Savings, 1966.

or more owned a television set. Even among the least well-off cohort, those earning less than 300,000 yen per year, while only one household in four had a refrigerator, more than 80 percent had a television. Nor was television ownership limited to the urban areas. Even if they could not afford any other consumer durables, people bought television sets.

Television sets were added to the CPI basket of goods and services in 1960, five years after washing machines. Among the other items added to the CPI basket that year were electric rice cookers, toasters, refrigerators, lipstick, cameras, and the NHK television subscription fee.

The Diffusion of Consumer Durables

Perhaps not as dramatic as the spread of television sets and washing machines, more or less the same story could be told about numerous other consumer durables. Figure 3 shows how the diffusion rates for a range of consumer durables in urban and rural areas changed over the years from 1959 to 1967. As might be expected, the urban areas were earlier adopters for most consumer durables. There are two reasons for this. Not only were these new products first shown and advertised in the urban areas, as with the television sets put out for public viewing, the urban lifestyle was less convention-bound and hence more open to adopting these life-changing products. As Amano Masako pointed out in her coauthored 2003 account of "women and things" in postwar Japan:

> Not only were there still major disparities between the urban and the rural areas in living standards and how people perceived their lives, there were considerable age and gender disparities in the rural areas in how receptive people were to the electrification of home life. Indeed, there are numerous accounts of bitter arguments over whether or not to get a washing machine. . . .
>
> Nor was this only a family affair, as people also had to do battle with village traditions and many a young couple could not buy a washing machine even if they wanted to unless they could win over the old women who argued, "Life was hard for us when we were young, so there's no reason you young ones should have it so easy." Even if the young wife wanted to get a washing machine, she would end up having to defer to her mother-in-law, who would argue that these newfangled

Figure 3. Ownership of consumer durables, urban vs rural, 1959–67

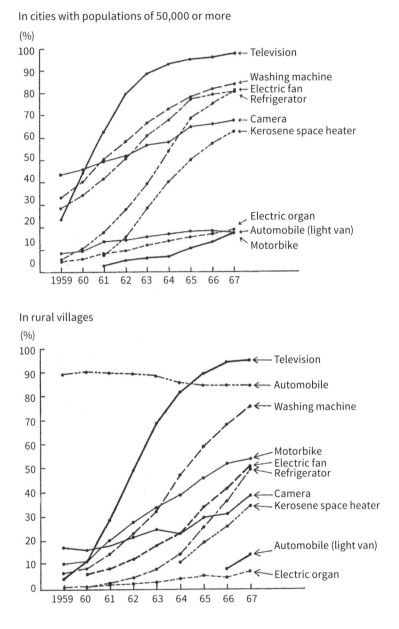

In cities with populations of 50,000 or more

(%)

- ← Television
- Washing machine
- ← Electric fan
- ← Refrigerator
- ← Camera
- ← Kerosene space heater
- Electric organ
- ← Automobile (light van)
- Motorbike

1959 60 61 62 63 64 65 66 67

In rural villages

(%)

- ← Television
- ← Automobile
- ← Washing machine
- ← Motorbike
- ← Electric fan
- ← Refrigerator
- ← Camera
- ← Kerosene space heater
- ← Automobile (light van)
- ← Electric organ

1959 60 61 62 63 64 65 66 67

Source: Economic Planning Agency, Trends of Consumption and Savings, 1966.

contraptions wasted water, would insist the young wife could not be trusted to do the laundry right, and would suspect she just wanted to get a machine to do the work so she could shirk her duties. One appliance manufacturer advertised its washing machines as wonderful devices that would free up time for young wives to read, but this was an impossible dream in many households.
(Amano Masako and Sakurai Atsushi, *"Mono to onna" no sengo-shi* [Heibonsha, 2003])

People did not face this level of resistance in the urban areas, where there were more nuclear families of just a young couple and their children and even one-person households. Little wonder the idea that the urban air set you free soon became a cliché.

This was most certainly a factor explaining why consumer durables tended to be adopted first in the urban areas and then to spread out from there. Yet psychological factors are not the whole story: another very important reason was that urban salaried employees' incomes tended to be higher than rural incomes. During the chaotic years immediately after the war's end, there was, it is true, a period when rural incomes were higher. Yet that disparity had largely disappeared by 1950, and urban incomes outpaced rural incomes in subsequent years. By 1960, the average annual income for an urban working household was 490,000 yen, about 23 percent more than the 400,000 figure for the average farming family. This difference made a difference. (The urban household figure is from the government's Family Income and Expenditure Survey, the rural household figure from its Survey of Farm Household Economy.)

The Changing Cityscape

About the same time as the diffusion of consumer durables was radically changing life at home, the cities were also undergoing a major transformation. Tokyo's successful bid to host the 1964 Olympic Games had a decisive impact that quickly went national.

In 1959, Tokyo was selected to host the 1964 Olympic Games. As soon as this was decided, the call went out: Now that the Olympics are coming to Tokyo, it is imperative Tokyo have the kind of environment and infrastructure of which we need not be ashamed. (See, for example, volume 6 of the Tokyo Metropolitan Government's centennial history of the capital, *Tōkyō hyakunenshi* [1979].) This simple desire was the impetus for the next half decade's efforts to create a city—indeed, to create a country—that everyone could be proud of. "Something we can be proud of" was, in fact, the unspoken core motive of the whole rapid-growth movement.

As the Olympics approached, the pace of building construction accelerated and contactors worked feverishly to complete new roads and widen existing ones. Streetcars, which had been the workhorse of the public transit infrastructure since before the war, continued to be phased out in favor of buses and taxicabs and were treated as nuisances in the rush to motorize. When the Tokyo Metropolitan Government set limits on automobile horns with a 1958 ordinance banning excessive noise, it also eliminated four of Tokyo's urban streetcar lines, including the popular line connecting Toranomon and Shinbashi 1-chome, the reasoning being that these lines were significant sources of noise pollution because drivers were blowing their horns at the pokey trolley cars, which averaged only 13 kilometers per hour. From the streetcars' perspective, this was a strange perversion of logic, but that was the way it happened. Correspondingly, the number of people riding the streetcars peaked in 1955 and declined thereafter as tracks were torn out and service was suspended in line with the Construction Ministry's "Streetcars are a nuisance. Get rid of them." thinking.

Meanwhile, the number of automobiles in Tokyo jumped from 240,000 in 1955 to 500,000 in 1959, 1.0 million in 1964, and 1.7 million in 1968, effectively doubling every four or five years. And of course, there was massive investment in building and improving the highway network to accommodate the advance of motorization. Epitomizing this was the construction of Tokyo's toll expressways.

It also needs to be mentioned here that this process included filling in or covering many of Tokyo's canals and other waterways. Waterways had been primary transport routes in Edo (as Tokyo was formerly known) for centuries. Even as the Great Kantō Earthquake of 1923 marked a major logistical turning point, rivers and canals continued to be important through the war years, especially in the low-lying *shitamachi* areas. One has only to look at the number of famous bridges (*-bashi*)—Kanda-bashi, Kamakura-bashi, Tokiwa-bashi, Ichikoku-bashi, Nihon-bashi, Edo-bashi, Kabuto-bashi, Chiyoda-bashi, Shimba-bashi, Kyūan-bashi, Takara-bashi, Danjō-bashi, Shintomi-bashi, Yanagi-bashi, Benkei-bashi, and more—to understand how central waterways were.

Filling in these waterways was also convenient for disposing of all of the rubble generated by the war and was thus perceived as a win-win measure by many. Not only was the rubble disposed of, but public works spending was justified, and Tokyo quickly jumped on this facile bandwagon to fill in and pave over many of its famed rivers and canals. As new public land, these land-filled ex-waterways then became prime candidates for new road construction, both at ground level and elevated. Seeking to build an expressway network of eight spokes radiating out from the center and several circumferential loops connecting them, Tokyo established the Metropolitan Expressway Public Corporation in June 1959, a mere three weeks after Tokyo was selected to host the 1964 Olympic Games.

The thinking was that any city with as many people as Tokyo is bound to have major traffic volume, motorization is inevitable, and ex-waterways are the easiest places to build new roads. Building upon these assumptions, it was decided that an expressway had to be built over historic Nihonbashi—creating an eyesore that endures even today. Looking at other great cities around the world, it is clear that this logic was wanting. There are, for example, no expressways over the Seine in Paris. Yet it was characteristic of Tokyo's mad rush to build more roadways that cultural and other considerations were ignored. Simplistic logic ruled.

The filling in of waterways and the construction of more and more paved roadways quickly changed the cityscape. This was not only the construction of new roads. Old roads also came in for widening and upgrading in line with the decision to prioritize motorization. Tree-lined streets lost their trees and the streetcars' safety islands were demolished. Neighborhood lanes where children once played were soon given over to vehicular traffic.

How did people react to all of these changes? Mostly with a sense of amazement and awe. I was still in elementary school at the time, but I remember the picture of an American elevated expressway interchange that graced our social studies textbook frontispiece and the wonder at seeing much the same thing being built right before my very eyes. And now I feel there are major problems with having just gaped open-mouthed as rampant motorization went unchecked.

Along with the roads, there was also a rush of new building construction, such as hotels. The Palace Hotel, Hotel Okura, and Hotel New Otani were all built between 1961 and 1964 in preparation for the Olympic visitors. Nor was the construction rush limited to Tokyo. Many of the iconic buildings in other cities throughout Japan were built during this same period. Adding subway construction to the mix, Tokyo was basically one vast construction site with workers swarming everywhere every day in the early 1960s. Even in the second half of the decade, after the Olympics were over, Tokyo embarked upon a heavy round of skyscraper construction that was echoed nationwide and continues to this very day. Following hard on the heels of the 36-story Kasumigaseki Building that was completed in 1968, a full score of high-rises were open for occupancy by the end of 1969. Also in 1969, plans were laid for creating urban subcenters in Tokyo. As part of this grand design, it was decided to move Tokyo's metropolitan government headquarters from their central location near Tokyo Station to the area west of Shinjuku Station, where a number of skyscrapers opened just a few years later. In large part, the Tokyo cityscape as we know it today was put in place by the mid-1970s.

Danchi and Modern Living

While the rapid-growth era may be best remembered for its office buildings and hotels, *danchi* (public apartment complexes) were also an important part of the construction program. The urban housing situation was, as described earlier, nothing short of abysmal right after the war. People who flooded into the urban areas during that chaotic period were lucky to find lodgings in barracks-like wooden apartment buildings, most of which offered only a single small room (typically about 10 square meters) in which to eat and sleep. Some 38 percent of Tokyo's housing was such wooden rental apartments in 1968, and these private-sector apartments housed a full quarter of the city's population. Thus it was that people set their sights on living in a *danchi*.

These *danchi* were complexes of standardized apartment buildings with each apartment having two or three rooms in addition to a kitchen big enough to double as a dining room—what became known as the *dainingu-kitchin* (dining room + kitchen), or DK for short. This was a new concept for many at the time. True, there had been concrete-construction apartment buildings (e.g., the Dōjunkai Apartments) even before the war, but the now-ubiquitous DK was a postwar innovation. Until then, meals had been prepared in the kitchen, carried out to another room, and put on low tables, the *chabudai*, to be eaten by diners sitting on the tatami-mat floor. Living in Tokyo in the 1950s as a child (I was born in 1951), I remember the whole family sitting around the *chabudai* when we ate. As shown in Figure 4, it was not until 1970 or so,

A typical *danchi* in Hibarigaoka near Tokyo visited by the Prince and Princess.
(© Kyodo News)

basically when the rapid-growth period ended, that tables and chairs replaced *chabudai* and tatami. Other innovations that the *danchi* brought to urban life in Japan included flush toilets, gas-heated baths, and south-facing balconies.

The typical *danchi* had several dozen—sometimes over a hundred—low-rise apartment buildings, and in this respect, too, differed from the prewar Dōjunkai Apartments. In the early 1980s, I lived in a housing project for civil service personnel in Osaka. The walls were unfinished concrete that had deteriorated conspicuously and the whole complex of buildings was in terrible condition. Shortly after I got there, the caretaker proudly told me it had been built as a prototype before the Tokyo Olympics and a lot of very important people from the Ministry of Education had come to see it when it was new. Given the condition it was in, I was not sure if I should have been pleased or disappointed to hear this. Yet during the rapid-growth years, the *danchi* were the very epitome of modern living.

Many other new consumer goods that showed up in Japan during this

A typical 1964 extended family having dinner at their *chabudai*. (Photo by Kageyama Kōyō)

Figure 4. Type of table for dining, 1920–82

(Survey of 300 households)

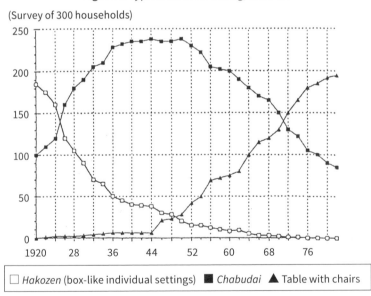

☐ *Hakozen* (box-like individual settings) ■ *Chabudai* ▲ Table with chairs

Source: Inoue Tadashi, "Shokutaku seikatsu-shi no chōsa to bunseki," in Ishige Nao-michi and Inoue Tadashi, eds., *Gendai Nihon ni okeru katei to shokutaku: Meimeizen kara chabudai e, Bulletin of the National Museum of Ethnology,* Special Issue 16, 1991.

era may not have been as conspicuously revolutionary as washing machines, refrigerators, and television sets, but they absolutely transformed Japanese food, shelter, and clothing, and hence the whole of Japanese life. Memorable in the food category was the advent of "instant" foods. Launched in 1958, Nissin Foods' trademarked "Chikin [Chicken] Rāmen" was the first of a long line of instant ramen products that were subsequently developed and marketed. By 1966, Nissin and others were selling 3 billion packets of instant ramen a year. Assuming a population of 100 million, this works out to every Japanese person eating a packet of instant ramen every 12 days or so. Other instant foods, such as instant coffee, *chāhan* (fried rice) mixes, and even pudding mixes soon followed.

The rapid-growth era was a time when everything changed from slow to fast, from dark to light. This was reflected even in the advertising jingles. For example,

Matsushita Electric's 1955 jingle for its National brand:

A-ka-ru-i Na-sho-na-ru	Look how bright, it's National
A-ka-ru-i Na-sho-na-ru	Look how bright, it's National
Mi-n-na i-e-jū de-n-ki de u-go-ku	Everything in the house is electric
A-ka-ru-i Na-sho-na-ru	Look how bright, it's National.

Or Toshiba's 1961 jingle:

Hi-ka-ru hi-ka-ru Tō-shi-ba	Shine on, shine on, Toshiba
Ma-wa-ru ma-wa-ru Tō-shi-ba	Round and round, it's Toshiba
Ha-shi-ru ha-shi-ru Tō-shi-ba	Run and run, it's Toshiba
U-ta-u u-ta-u Tō-shi-ba	Sing and sing, it's Toshiba
Ka-ga-ya-ku hi-ka-ri hi-ka-ri	See how bright, how bright it shines
Tsu-yo-i chi-ka-ra chi-ka-ra	See how strong, how strong it is
Mi-n-na mi-n-na Tō-shi-ba	Each and everybody's Toshiba
Tō-shi-ba no mā-ku	The Toshiba badge.

People's tastes and dietary habits also changed. Rice consumption peaked and bread became increasingly popular. Consumption of such formerly exotic vegetables as tomatoes and lettuce grew, as did meat consumption. People began to prefer fatty foods to the traditional lean diet. As Hattori Yukio's dictionary of culinary ingredients *Shokuzai jiten* (Fuji TV Publishing, 1995) describes it:

In the Edo period, tuna [*maguro*] was considered an inferior fish, something to be salted and stored for eating in an emergency. Perhaps surprisingly it was only in the middle of the Meiji era [in the very late nineteenth century] that people developed a taste for tuna sashimi and tuna slowly became accepted as suitable for sushi. But even then, tuna was considered a low-brow sushi, and *toro* [the fatty cuts] was considered something to be thrown away—something not even the cat would eat—because nobody liked the oily taste. Yet following the Tokyo Olympics and the spreading acceptance of Western foods, people found that fatty foods could also taste good and *toro* came to be considered a prime sushi cut. In the late 1960s, this fatty tuna became an accepted part of the Japanese diet. In the longer span of things, it is a very recent addition.

Food tastes change over time, but Japanese people's lives changed in many other ways: from tatami to wooden floors, from *chabudai* to tables, from futon to beds, and from rice to bread. Indeed, the changes during the rapid-growth era were equivalent to those during the time of Japan's cultural opening to the West following the 1868 Meiji Restoration—changes epitomized by the Rokumeikan (Deer Cry Pavilion) of the 1880s.

The Izanagi Boom and the End of the Rapid-Growth Era

By the mid-1960s, over 80 percent of households had washing machines, television sets, and refrigerators—previously characterized as the three sacred treasures—and some people thought the sociocultural revolution would plateau. At this juncture, what should appear but the "three Cs": a *car*, a *color* television, and an air *conditioner*. These three had their Japanese debut in the late 1960s, pushing the sociocultural revolution forward just as the earlier trio seemed to be running out of steam. All three were added to the CPI basket of goods and services in 1970. The automobile in particular had an immeasurable impact on Japan's economy and society, one that has continued to the present. As of 1967, only 6.6 percent of farming families and only 7.5 percent of urban employed households owned a car, but 63 percent of rural households and 39 percent of urban households had at least one person with a driver's license. In the late 1960s, the phrase *maikā* (my car) was popularized to express people's desire to own their own family car, and the groundwork was laid for the age of motorization.

Washing the family car. (© Kyodo News)

The advent of the three Cs and other new consumer durables pushed the revolution in Japanese life to a new level. The Japanese economy had already experienced the Jinmu Boom (December 1954 to June 1957), so named because it was said to be the strongest burst of economic growth since the days of the legendary Emperor Jinmu, and then the Iwato Boom (July 1958 to December 1961). These were then followed by the 57-month expansion (the longest ever recorded) that lasted from 1965 into 1970, which was dubbed the Izanagi Boom. Having run through several notable names from Japanese mythology, the rapid-growth era finally found closure with Izanagi the creator.

The consumer lifestyle revolution during this period was very much characterized by Americanization. From the 1950s through the early 1960s, "modern living" was the touchstone, but looking back, it was a very primitive modern. By contrast, the Izanagi Boom brought modernization that still holds luster even today. In apparel, for example, market leadership shifted away from practical utility and passed to expressive fashion. Created largely by Ōhashi Ayumi, the covers of the weekly magazine *Heibon Punch* (first published in April 1964) were largely depictions of American fashions, music, and other things that appealed to young men. Young people became familiar with the *aibī* (Ivy League) look and started buying preppy-style shirts and sweaters from VAN Jacket Inc. They also took to wearing jeans. The styles that were popular with young men then are not that different from what we commonly see today.

The changes in women's fashions were more dramatic. The miniskirt look that came to Japan in the fall of 1967 with the British model Twiggy spread like a flash among the large cohort of young women born during Japan's postwar baby boom. Hems 15 centimeters above the knee were symbolic of the spirit of the times. It was also in the fall of 1967 that Renown's "YeYe" brand of knitwear captured the market with a catchy jingle and attractive full-color visuals on television.

In 1964, Japan graduated to International Monetary Fund (IMF) Article VIII status and overseas travel was liberalized. This did not mean that everyone started globe-trotting. A full-package 17-day trip to Europe was available, but it was priced at about twice the average annual pay of an entry-level salaried employee. At the same time, currency controls remained in place, and the maximum a resident was allowed to take overseas was 500 US dollars. Almost all overseas travel was on business. In fact, Japanese people took a total of only 210,000 trips overseas in 1964 (including multiple trips by the same people). This had, however, increased to 2.2 million by 1973—a 10-fold increase in as many years. Assuming no multiple trips, this 2.2 million figure out of a population of about 100 million would mean that one in 50 Japanese traveled overseas in 1973—something that would have been inconceivable 10 years earlier. While it is perhaps unreasonable to compare this to the situation as of 2012, when currency exchange rate fluctuations have resulted in the dollar's being worth only 80-some yen and have thus made international travel readily accessible to ordinary Japanese, it is nonetheless worth noting the substantial increase that took place in the decade following 1964, when the dollar was still 360 yen.

Similar stories could be told about almost anything. The Izanagi Boom years in the late 1960s were a major force in shaping Japanese life as we now know it. In the three years from 1966 through 1968, Japan surpassed the UK, France, and West Germany, one a year, to become the second-largest Western economy (trailing only the United States) and an economic power in its own right.

Even though the rapid-growth years ended as the Izanagi Boom wound down, in less than 20 years starting in the mid-1950s, Japan had become a totally different country in socioeconomic terms. We are now about four decades past that, but Japanese life today is not much different from what it was in the early 1970s. If you went out in the early 1970s, you saw people wearing jeans and eating hamburgers at McDonald's—the same as today. The changes that took place in a mere 6,000 days between 1955 and 1970 were far more extensive and far more significant than anything that has happened in the 40 years since.

China's Rapid Growth

The link between rapid economic growth and the diffusion of consumer durables does not just hold in Japan. It is thus worth taking a quick look at rapid economic growth as it has played out in China.

With the start of the reform and opening-up policies announced by Deng Xiaoping in late 1978, the Chinese economy achieved GDP growth of over 10 percent per year. While the Engel's coefficient showing how much of the consumer budget went to foodstuffs remained high and was greater than 50 percent into the 1990s—not much different from the case of Japan in the 1950s before the start of rapid growth—the diffusion of consumer durables tracked economic growth in China much the same as it had in Japan.

In 1981, urban employed household ownership of washing machines was 6.3 percent, and the figure for refrigerators a mere 0.2 percent. Four years later, these ownership ratios had shot up to 48.3 percent and 6.6 percent, respectively. By 2004, virtually all urban employed households (96 percent) owned washing machines. As in Japan, the rapid spread of consumer durable ownership was fueled in no small part by rising urban household incomes.

Unsurprisingly, the diffusion of consumer durables was much slower in rural villages, where incomes are only about one-third what they are in the cities. Even as late as 2010, about 40 percent of China's employed labor force was rural, and consumer durable ownership was correspondingly lower. Yet as rural incomes rise, so does the ownership of appliances. In the case of some items, notably mobile phones, ownership is already very widespread. (In 2004, the mobile phone ownership ratio was 111.4 percent.) Given China's population of over 1.3 billion, one can only wonder what electricity demand will be like when everyday life is fully modernized and how China will meet the greater energy demand consequent upon still-further motorization.

China's GDP outstripped Japan's in 2010, making it the second-largest economic power in the world. But China's population is 13 times Japan's, and its per capita income is still only about a tenth of Japan's. This gap is really the driving force behind China's rapid economic growth. While its rapid growth will also wind down at some point, China is today firmly embarked upon the same rapid growth trajectory that Japan traveled earlier.

CHAPTER 3
Technological Innovation and Corporate Management

Kawasaki Steel's Chiba Works. (© Kyodo News)

New products debuted one after another to totally change Japanese life during the rapid-growth years. And once released, these products got cheaper and cheaper every year. Whether it was washing machines, television sets, or anything else, these new consumer goods that started out priced beyond the ordinary household's reach quickly fell in price and became generally affordable. Both the new products and the price slippage can be attributed to technological innovation.

Joseph Schumpeter, one of the great economic thinkers of the twentieth century, and one many rank right alongside John Maynard Keynes, used the term *innovation* to cover (1) developing a new product or a new production technology, (2) developing a new market, (3) developing a new source of the raw materials needed, and (4) developing and utilizing a new organizational model. When swarms of enterprises appear seeking the enhanced profits that accrue from successful innovation, this creates "good" economic conditions and is the prime mover behind capitalist economic growth. Or so Schumpeter explained it.

The 1956 Economic White Paper authored by Gotō Yonosuke—a government economist nicknamed "Mr. White Paper"—strongly endorsed Schumpeter's emphasis on innovation and technological progress, contending in its conclusion:

> The speed with which the postwar Japanese economy recovered was something that truly nobody could have foreseen. It was driven by the convergence of hard work by all of the people and facilitated by favorable conditions overseas.
>
> That said, it should not be forgotten how deep was the abyss into which Japan had fallen, nor that its very depth enabled Japan to claw its

way back up so quickly. There were a number of factors involved. At the economic policy level, it was sufficient to take care to avoid serious deterioration in the balance of payments and to not fall prey to deleterious inflation. Consumers needed to be constantly open to purchasing new things and industry constantly open to investing new funds. At present, given the state of our economic recovery, we have pretty much exhausted this updraft. Admittedly, Japan is still poor and may well have more consumer and investment potential than some other countries, but there has been an unmistakable decline in this burning desire to consume and to invest from what it was at one point after the war. Our postwar is over, and we have entered a new phase. Recovery-mediated growth is over, and future growth will be sustained by our efforts to modernize.

The white paper went on to explicate this modernization:

> In discussing the global economy, we earlier explained that technological innovation is a major sustainment for economic growth. We talk about technological innovation, but, as seen above, this is a wide-ranging process encompassing even the structure of consumption. Overseas, innovation has been further expanded to embrace both technological advances and the transformational changes that take place in the nation's economy in response to the restructuring of effective demand that accompanies these technological advances. Among the manifestations typically cited as resulting from this transformation are more sophisticated production modalities, changes in the relationship between raw materials and finished products, the development of new products and the shift in consumption patterns to services and consumer durables, a shift in trade patterns linked to more sophisticated domestic industry, and a redistribution of human resources as labor moves from less productive sectors to more productive sectors. In addition, and in response to the new global circumstances, it has come to be considered that moves to assist the developing countries with their development are also part of this phenomenon. We have chosen to call this transformation the modernization of our economic structure.

Written at the start of the rapid-growth era, this white paper was extremely prescient about how the Japanese economy would develop. The idea of technological innovation is indeed a key concept for understanding not only the rapid-growth era but the Japanese economy as a whole.

Flourishing Technological Innovation

It is the enterprise that is responsible for innovation. Many new enterprises sprang up one after another in the youthful exuberance of newfound freedoms right after the war. Sony (originally Tōkyō Tsūshin Kōgyō) was established in 1946, the year after the war ended, Honda in 1948, and Sanyo in 1950. These are just a few of the outstanding companies that were established in this period and went on to be among the best in Japan. In all of these companies, it was the engineers who took the lead and brought in the new technology needed to produce their dream products. Morita Akio, a Sony founder, explained it in his book *Made in Japan*:

> As new-product quality and reliability and advancement become commonplace, we in industry are challenged to create things that will be new and intriguing enough to bring the customers to us. Obviously, we can never expect to survive in business if we do not keep improving what we offer to the public, and that takes new technology.
> (Morita Akio et al., *Made in Japan* ([E. P. Dutton, 1986], 239)

This same entrepreneurial spirit drove many companies. Nor was it only the new enterprises that were alert to new technologies. Major corporations were also very active in licensing new foreign technologies and developing new technologies of their own. Toray, for example, spent an enormous sum of money to license nylon technology from DuPont in 1951 and Nissan Motors entered into a wide-ranging technical tie-up with the Austin Motor Company in 1952. Kawasaki Steel's decision to build its massive Chiba Works is perhaps the best example of these major firms' proactive management. Kawasaki had just been a steel company buying pig iron and making it into steel with their open-hearth furnaces, but they quickly announced plans in 1950 to create one of the most advanced integrated steel plants in the world by adding two 500-ton-class blast furnaces, six 100-ton-class open hearth furnaces, and two rolling mills in world-class continuous mills. This new investment then gave them the capacity to produce 500,000 tons of crude steel a year, or about one-tenth of the total Japanese capacity of 5.3 million tons per year. While Bank of Japan Governor Ichimada Hisato derided this plan, saying the site would end up as just another field of weeds, Kawasaki's Chiba Works defied the naysayers' expectations by firing up its first blast furnace in 1953, thus getting a running start on meeting the expanding demand for steel, being among the first mills to reap the transportation advantages of a littoral location, and demonstrating the need for the latest technology. Kawasaki was ahead of the curve on this.

Starting in 1955 and continuing throughout the rapid-growth period management was generally very positive about the benefits of adopting the latest technology. As part of this mindset, the Japan Productivity Center was established in 1955. While it was the business sector that took the initiative in establishing the Center, the idea was to encourage labor involvement from the very start, and the Center worked to promote good labor relations. The basic premise was that of labor and management cooperating to enhance productivity and then distributing the gains from that enhanced productivity equitably based upon labor-management consultations. Labor initially rejected this approach outright. In 1956, for example, the Yawata Iron & Steel union campaign called for "opposing productivity enhancements at labor's expense." Yet by 1960, the same union was saying "Fight for a share of the efficiency gains." Productivity enhancement—often termed efficiency or rationalization—moved from being seen as an evil that would cost people their jobs to being seen as a good thing that benefited both labor and management, and this cooperative approach is one of the Japanese economy's strengths to this day.

The adoption of printing automation in the newspaper industry was one of the major success stories building upon the labor-management accord developed during the rapid-growth years. Newspapers started to make use of computer technology in the 1960s. Kanji (logographic characters) were a major obstacle in the early stages, but all of the newspaper companies devoted considerable resources to this task in pursuit of the major productivity gains that could be achieved if the papers could computerize their editing and layout. Along with the technical issues involved, there were also potential stumbling blocks in the workplace, but labor and management worked together to overcome these legacy issues with reassignments, on-the-job training, and other measures in lieu of layoffs. As a result, most Japanese newspapers were completely computerized by the early 1980s.

The British case stands in striking contrast. When *The Times* of London moved to computerize its printing operations in 1986, they encountered major labor pushback. High-paid printers rejected the effort nationwide, and the publisher struck back by firing the entire union membership and barring union members from its Wapping plant. In retaliation, other sympathetic workers blocked the shipment of newspapers from the printing plant, the police were called in, and there was bloodshed. Japan's case could have been equally tragic had it not been for the generally good labor-management relations engendered during the rapid-growth era.

The steel industry was so crucial to the economy in the rapid-growth years that it was sometimes said Japan was "steel country." It is thus worth looking at the impact of technological innovation and restructuring in the steel industry. Technological innovation in the steel industry in the 1950s and 1960s may be roughly divided into four half-decade periods. The first phase (1951–55) was when Kawasaki Steel built its Chiba Works with more modern rolling mills and bigger open-hearth furnaces. Approximately 70 percent of the new equipment that was needed for this phase's efficiency gains was imported.

The second phase of this rationalization centered on the Linz-Donawitz (LD) basic oxygen converter process for steel. This technological innovation in steelmaking was proved at the LD steelworks in Austria and offered a far superior technology for steelmaking than the traditional open-hearth method. The first reports of success with the LD process were reported in the German steel industry journal *Stahl und Eisen* in December 1950. The first people in Japan to notice the report were engineers at Nippon Kōkan. Engineers at U.S. Steel and other American firms initially ignored this revolutionary new technology because they were proud of the technology they already had and did not believe a region they had recently vanquished could develop better technology. While it also took time to win over the skeptics in Japan, the major Japanese steelmakers moved to adopt LD technology in the late 1950s, leading with Yawata in 1957 and Nippon Kōkan in 1958. This was about half a decade before U.S. Steel's 1963 move, and this lead was an important factor in the Japanese industry's staking out a position of global leadership—something that would have been unthinkable a decade earlier.

By the early 1960s, all of the leading steel companies were building large-scale integrated works in littoral locations, including Kimitsu (in Chiba) and Ōita. This trend was further accelerated with the Izanagi Boom in the late 1960s. Complementing these siting decisions was the birth of "hyperworks" capable of producing up to 10 million tons of raw steel in a single year. Indeed, "economies of scale" was a popular subject in management circles at this time, as epitomized by the merger of Yawata Steel and Fuji Steel in 1970 to form today's Nippon Steel behemoth.

In the 1970s, approximately two decades after Kawasaki Steel built its Chiba Works, Japan surpassed the United States as the world leader in steel technology. In terms of raw steel output, Japan was shoulder to shoulder with the United States and the Soviet Union as one of the three largest producers in 1973 at over 100 million tons per year. Ironically, it was just about this same time that the oil crisis of 1973–74 erupted and threw the steel industry into worldwide turmoil. That is, however, another story for another book.

The Japanese steel industry continued to provide high-quality steel at low cost throughout the rapid-growth period thanks to the industry's faith in and zest for technological innovation. And it was this high-quality, low-cost steel that made possible the diffusion of the washing machines, television sets, automobiles, and other consumer durables that so changed Japanese life. This steel was also used in the construction of mammoth tankers, a contributing factor in the energy revolution discussed below.

Lest there be any doubt, it is worth quantifying just how successful the steel industry's technological innovation was. Table 4 shows the hours of labor needed to produce one ton of pig iron or steel. Obviously, the fewer hours needed, the better the labor productivity. The inverses of the numbers in Table 4 indicate how much steel can be produced per hour of labor, which is a direct measure of productivity.

From 1951 to 1958, the amount of labor needed to produce a ton of blast-furnace steel approximately halved, which is to say labor productivity approximately doubled. In contrast, labor productivity at open-hearth furnaces improved by only 40 percent or so. More significantly, when the LD process was introduced in 1960, it started out needing just 0.75 hours per ton, or less than half the 1.54 hours per ton needed in open-hearth furnaces, and this productivity was doubled by 1970. Blast furnace productivity also got consistently better (nearly four times better) over the course of the decade. On the other hand, open-hearth furnaces, which had been the mainstay until blast furnaces were introduced, showed no productivity gains—and in fact showed productivity loss—in the 1960s, indicating what an obsolete technology it was. Looking at Table 4 overall, it is clear that productivity in the steel industry improved 10-fold over the two decades shown. This was the result of technological innovation.

Table 4. Labor productivity in the steel industry (hours per ton of production)

	Blast furnace	Open hearth	Oxygen converter
1951	1.77	3.01	--
1952	1.71	2.93	--
1953	1.45	2.68	--
1954	1.36	2.46	--
1955	1.252	2.12	--
1956	1.07	2.00	--
1957	0.98	1.85	--
1958	0.91	1.83	--
1959	0.75	1.69	--
1960	0.66	1.54	0.75
1961	0.53	1.46	0.60
1962	0.48	1.57	0.68
1963	0.44	1.56	0.58
1964	0.38	1.36	0.48
1965	0.35	1.60	0.48
1966	0.30	1.62	0.42
1967	0.25	1.52	0.38
1968	0.21	1.72	0.38
1969	0.17	1.60	0.34
1970	0.16	1.87	0.34

Source: Ministry of Labor, Labor Productivity Statistics Survey Report.
Note: Labor productivity here is measured as the hours of work in the direct process, not including transport, raw materials, inspection, reworking, and the like.

The fruits of technological innovation were not, of course, limited to labor productivity. New materials and new parts and components also became available. Yet for these new parts and components to be useful, there had to be a sufficient market for the new products they were used in. The transistor, which was invented in the 1950s, provides an apt example. It is impossible to discuss transistor production in Japan without also touching upon the development of the transistor radio. Without the transistor radio and similar products, the transistor itself would never have been anything more than a laboratory novelty. With the start of commercial radio broadcasts in 1951, the transistor radio's popularity soared, and soon nearly everyone had one. It was also about this time that Sony started developing its overseas markets and the transistor radio became an important export. Transistor production made transistor radio production possible, and the strong market for transistor radios then ensured the transistor became a significant industry in its own right.

A similar process played out with integrated circuits (ICs) and small desktop calculators in the late 1960s as the rapid-growth era was drawing to a close. The IC was invented in 1959 and was deployed almost entirely for military use in the United States. As a result, it was assumed IC technology would not find fertile ground in Japan, which had no military to speak of. Yet the market for small desktop calculators—only a niche market elsewhere—took off with explosive force in Japan, with the market for these small calculators in turn feeding back and driving further developments in IC technology. Even after Japan's rapid growth died down, global markets entered the age of electronics in the 1970s and ICs were considered an industrial staple. The foundations for this process were laid by the strong market that Japan sustained for small calculators.

Investment Begets Investment

As noted above, the benefits of technological innovation were all made manifest with new machinery and other plant investment, which is to say they required investment. The switch to gigantic blast furnaces and the LD process, and the construction of sprawling littoral industrial complexes—these are just some of the many capital investments that were needed. As such, it may justifiably be said that the rapid-growth period, driven as it was by technological innovation, was a period of investment-led growth.

As the steel industry continued to innovate in technology for rolling sheet steel, the price of steel sheeting went down and the quality went up, which in turn had a major impact on the price and quality of household appliances (white goods), automobiles, and other steel-using consumer products; the lower prices in turn accelerating the diffusion of washing machines, television sets, automobiles, and the like, as already noted.

Growing demand for appliances, automobiles, and the like created demand for capacity-enhancing investment in these industries, which in turn generated demand for the equipment used on the production lines and hence demand for investment in the equipment and machinery industries. As part of this, the enhanced demand for consumer durables and automobiles generated demand for such new materials as rubber tires and synthetic resins, which stimulated investment in the petrochemical industries. And the robust capital investment in all of these different industries then redounded to demand for ever-larger blast furnaces, integrated steel mills along the coastlines, and other investment in and by the steel industry.

In effect, technological innovation and investment in the steel industry and other "upstream" industries contributed to lower prices and better quality in such "downstream" industries as household appliances and automobiles, boosting demand there and forcing companies to invest more in design, production, and sales facilities. At the same time, the increased demand downstream generated increased demand upstream and forced industries even further upstream to also invest more heavily in their core processes. This was the shape of the Japanese economy during the rapid-growth era, with interconnected industries growing together on the basis of strong consumer

Table 5. Capital investment in the petrochemical industry

	Ethylene production capacity (thousand tons)	Capital investment (million yen)	Actual investment index (base year 1970)
1956	0	8,349	3.3
1957	0	24,017	9.5
1958	43	23,396	9.9
1959	115	27,555	11.5
1960	115	38,494	15.9
1961	160	66,435	27.2
1962	316	55,904	23.3
1963	378	62,017	25.4
1964	633	91,229	37.3
1965	1,080	110,921	45.0
1966	1,190	77,202	30.6
1967	1,565	109,215	42.5
1968	1,970	202,837	78.3
1969	2,480	216,547	81.8
1970	4,010	274,299	100.0
1971	4,330	251,762	92.5
1972	4,980	152,467	55.6
1973	4,980	140,195	44.1
1974	5,065	240,818	57.7
1975	5,145	280,650	65.3
1976	5,185	226,853	50.0
1977	5,215	192,680	41.9
1978	5,235	110,643	24.7
1979	6,097	117,016	24.3
1980	6,257	200,614	35.4

Source: Watanabe Tokuji and Saeki Yasuharu, *Tenki ni tatsu sekiyu kagaku kōgyō* [The Petrochemical Industry at a Turning Point] (Iwanami Shoten, 1984).
Note: The actual investment index is the investment adjusted to take account of changes in the wholesale price index.

demand. The Economic White Paper for 1960 characterized this as "investment begetting investment," and this was true of the Japanese economy throughout the rapid-growth years.

Although a relative newcomer, the petrochemical industry was typical. As shown in Table 5, investment in the petrochemical industry grew more than 10-fold over the period from 1957 through its peak year in 1970. Yet it then fell by half in just a couple of years. This investment plunge preceded the oil crisis of 1973. All of this is important to understanding the end of the rapid-growth years and the mechanisms that sustained Japan's rapid growth, and we will return to this issue in Chapter 5.

The Changing Workplace

Naturally, all of this technological innovation also impacted employment and wages. Komatsu Hiroshi, who worked in human resources management at Shin-Nippon Steel for 40 years starting before the war (including the period when the company was known as Yawata Steel), has written about this. Until around the early 1950s, Komatsu recounted, "the criterion for someone who wanted a job in the steel industry was that they had to be strong enough to do heavy work and to endure the high temperatures in the workplace. Companies were not interested in academic ability so much as they were in the candidate's ability to heft a bale of rice, say." All of this changed as production was made more rational and more efficient in the late 1950s and early 1960s. Komatsu explained:

> Perhaps one of the most conspicuous changes in Japanese hiring practices during this period was the policy switch to hiring high school graduates. . . . In implementing the second round of technological innovations, hard on the heels of the first round, the steel industry realized that blast furnace technology was on the brink of extinction, that they might soon have to phase out all of their big blast furnaces, and that they really had to rethink their business model. This was a major turning point for the industry as a whole. However, even though they knew they had to engineer massive restructuring, they did not have the financial wherewithal to pull this off and had to go to the banks for financing. Then, once they were finally able to get the equipment and put this new technology in, they realized they needed better-educated

workers to get the most out of the technology. The old steelworkers who had come to the mills out of elementary school were hard workers imbued with a strong sense of loyalty to the company, but they were unable, for example, to make heads or tails of the instruction manuals that came with the new German equipment. Nor did they have the necessary grounding in electrical engineering to operate the control panels to best effect. The time was past when an experienced worker could just look at the color of the flame and tell if there was too much or too little phosphorous or whatever. The industry could no longer fly by the seat of its pants, and it needed people fully conversant with the equipment's navigational system. It needed better-educated workers.
(Interview with Komatsu Hiroshi, "Nihonteki koyō kankō o kizuita hitotachi: Komatsu Hiroshi ni kiku (2)," *Nihon Rōdō Kyōkai Zasshi*, March 1982)

Table 6, showing the ages and educational backgrounds of workers at plants where the rolling mill process was introduced in 1957, tends to substantiate what Komatsu said. With the increasing sophistication of the equipment used there was a definite industry-wide shift toward younger and better-educated workers. This does not, however, mean that all industries experienced this same sort of shift in their blue-collar workforces. The electrical equipment, automotive, and a few other industries are notable exceptions. At Toyota, for example, as shown in Table 7, junior high-school graduates continued to be the mainstay of the workforce (excluding part-timers) throughout the rapid-growth period.

The restructuring of the workplace that resulted from the technological innovation typified by the steel industry also affected the structure of wages—leading, for example, to the switch from wages based upon employment seniority to wages based upon the individual's specific job. The difficulties encountered were later summarized in a Nippon Steel corporate history citing the example of when the company was considering this switch in the fall of 1958. The explanation was in a section titled "Personnel and wage issues." It read, in part:

The new job responsibilities that arise as a result of technological innovation and other factors do not fit neatly into the broad administrative, engineering, operations, and other categories, with the result that there

Table 6. Age and educational level of workers in rolling mill operations, July 1960

		Old rolling mills	New rolling mills
Age	20 and under	0	0
	21–25	0	15
	26–30	3	19
	31–35	9	8
	36–40	13	4
	41–45	17	1
	46–50	3	0
	51 and over	5	0
	Total	50	47
Education	Upper elementary	50	21
	New junior high		6
	Old jr. high or new high school		3
	Vocational high school		17

Source: Ministry of Labor, *Rōdō Tōkei Chōsa Geppō* (Monthly Labor Research and Statistics Bulletin), December 1960.
Note: Data are from a Ministry of Labor survey of mills that put in new hot-strip rolling mill equipment in 1957.

Table 7. Educational background of new Toyota regular-employee hires

	New grad. school	Old univ. or grad. school	New university		Junior or vocational college	New high school		Jr. high school			Total	Hourly workers
			Male	Female		Male	Female	Nurse school	Male	Female		
1951												
1952						6					6	
1953		6	8			31		3	31		79	
1954	1		12			18		9	37		77	
1955			8		8	8		10	16		50	
1956			15			11		10	17		53	200
1957	3		34		1 (female)	19	22		54		133	362
1958	1	3	35		1 (female)	15	59	10	47	28	199	196
1959	1		38	3		30	31		82	28	213	1,465
1960	2		48	3		64	60	10	152	45	384	3,752
1961	1		55	5	3 (female)	122	96		230	64	576	3,366

Source: Japan Institute of Labor, "Nihonteki koyō kankō o kizuita hitotachi (2): Yamamoto Keimei-shi ni kiku (2)," *Nihon Rōdō Kyōkai Zasshi*, 1982.

is considerable overlap and confusion as to how to handle them. With the plant modernizing to keep up with technological innovation, the actual work performed by those on the operational front lines is changing (from manual labor to mental labor), meaning that the people also need to change and we need mainly high school graduates. Yet having better-educated people has in turn seemingly pitted them against the lower-grade clerical staff and made it important that uniform standards be established for status, pay, and other aspects. Especially with the changes in the actual work that the line people are doing, a disparity has developed between the wages paid people based upon their years of service (seniority) and the wages paid based upon the responsibilities and technical skills their jobs require.

Komatsu explained:

Assuming the younger high school graduates can read the foreign texts, can get the most out of the machinery, and work hard, it is clear that you cannot stay with the same seniority-based wages for the older workers forever. At the same time, however, it is also clear that switching to a work-based pay schedule all at once would mean some new high school graduates would be making more than the more experienced workers, which would negatively impact the older workers' loyalty and motivation. All of this was taken into careful consideration in moving to the job-based wage schedules.

As a result, the changes in the skill sets that technological innovation demanded had a major impact on how the company itself was structured.

More STEM Students

Because this technological innovation was driven and sustained by engineers, it sparked a sharp increase in demand for people with engineering skills. Responding to this in November 1957, the Ministry of Education announced a three-year program to enhance STEM (science, technology, engineering, and mathematics) education, increasing the number of STEM students at universities by 8,000. While this was obviously drawn up based on industrial needs, it should be noted that 1957 was the year the Soviet Union

Table 8. Enrollment in University of Tokyo faculties

	Engineering	Science	Law	Letters	Economics	Agriculture	Medicine
1959	453	132	645	326	309	195	93
1965	784	180	603	339	325	203	120
1967	845	205	625	340	321	194	116

Source: University of Tokyo, *Tōkyō Daigaku hyakunenshi*, vol. 3 of reference material (University of Tokyo Press, 1986).
Notes: Figures are single-year enrollment numbers estimated from total enrollment in each faculty. The smaller faculties of education and pharmaceutical sciences are not included.

put the world's first artificial satellite in orbit (Sputnik, in October), shocking the United States and setting off a worldwide clamor for more and better STEM education. Born as it was during an international STEM rush, Japan's 1957 push to increase the number of STEM students was later expanded, prompting the creation of new departments and the consolidation of existing departments at institutions of higher education throughout Japan. Table 8 shows how, for example, enrollment in the University of Tokyo's different departments changed over the years—with increases in the science and engineering departments, especially in engineering.

The push for more STEM education was not limited to universities. In 1962, the National Institutes of Technology were established, five-year schools combining the high school and junior college curricula to provide the education operational-level engineers needed. This new track started with a dozen schools and grew quickly throughout the 1960s in response to the clamor for more and more engineers. In this and other ways, the wave of technological innovation set off major changes in the very structure of Japanese higher education.

Of course, structural changes in the educational system should not be judged solely on how they impact the economy or the contributions they make to the material things that we can easily see. If you look, for example, at the European universities as they have existed since the Middle Ages, the so-called practical studies have not grown that much more significant, with the exception of a few fields such as medicine. Even in modern times, engineering and other "practical" fields center on non-university or extra-university research and educational institutions. In this respect, Japanese education may perhaps be said to be ahead of the Western curve in having emphasized practical subjects since well before the war.

How, then, are we to assess the push to expand STEM education in the early 1960s? As a start, it would be hard to deny that this shift was a major contributor to and sustainer of the technological innovation that took place in Japanese manufacturing, particularly of machinery, from the late 1960s on. Conversely, were there offsetting losses in Japanese education? While it is impossible to answer that difficult question here, it should be raised and borne in mind.

From Coal to Petroleum

The rapid-growth period also saw a shift in Japan's energy situation as the nation moved from coal to petroleum. Around 1950, shortly before the growth took off, over half of the Japanese people lived in rural villages and their most important energy source was kindling and charcoal they provided for themselves. Yet for the nation as a whole, coal was the primary source of energy for industry, trains, and urban living. After the war, Japan looked to coal and steel to pull itself out of its distressed situation. The Priority Production System adopted by the cabinet in December 1946 designated coal a priority sector entitled to special allocations of financial and other resources. The coal industry was a central player and mainstay of the Japanese economy, employing 350,000 people, or about one percent of the Japanese labor force, in 1950.

This industry was, however, quickly eclipsed in the early 1950s. Not only were a number of high-yield oil fields discovered in the Middle East during World War II, the advances in tanker technology slashed transport costs and made it possible to exploit these oil fields profitably. Coal, which was inferior to oil as an industrial energy source, soon found itself unable to compete with oil even in cost terms. By the late 1950s, coal was 30 percent more expensive per calorie than petroleum. The shift from coal to petroleum that started in the 1950s accelerated in the 1960s. Although coal still accounted for 41 percent of Japan's energy in 1960, it dropped to less than half that level in the 1970s. Nor was this shift evident only in Japan. Except for the United States, where petroleum was already a primary energy resource, Germany, Britain, the Soviet Union, and other countries all followed the same coal-to-oil trajectory as Japan.

Table 9. Primary energy sources (10^{12} kcal)

	Hydroelectric	Coal	Petroleum, LNG (imports)	Nuclear	Natural gas (domestic)	Total
1945	50.8	135.5	2.4	–	0.4	193.1
1950	92.6	234.9	28.7	–	0.7	401.9
1955	174.7	302.9	112.7	–	2.4	641.3
1960	157.8	415.2	379.3	–	9.4	1,008.1
1965	179.4	456.5	1,006.8	0.1	20.3	1,689.1
1970	178.9	635.7	2,298.9	10.5	39.7	3,197.1
1975	192.4	599.9	2,686.4	56.5	92.3	3,662.2

Source: From Table 4-11 in Yano Tsuneta Kinenkai, ed., *Sūji de miru Nihon no 100 nen*, 3rd ed. (Kokusei-sha, 1991), which draws upon *Sō enerugī tōkei* (Energy Statistics) by the Ministry of International Trade and Industry and *Denki jigyō binran* (Overview of Electric Power Operations) by the Federation of Electric Power Companies.

Inevitable though it may have been, the shift mandated by this energy revolution was not entirely smooth. Mining layoffs, mine closings, and bankruptcies started in the early 1950s and were soon followed by strikes protesting the downsizing, as well as a number of tragic mine accidents. All of this came together in the 1960 Miike dispute.

In 1959, Mitsui Mining announced a major overhawl that included wage cuts and early retirements that it said were needed to ensure the company's survival in the face of the harsh business climate. When fewer employees signed up for early retirement at Miike than at the company's five other mines, the company drew up a list of 1,200 people slated for early retirement, including the union leaders. It also imposed a lockout at the Miike mine in January 1960. In response, the union called an open-ended strike. Things continued in basic stalemate for over 280 days with serious clashes and bloodshed, and not even an injunction by the local court or a finding by the arbitration board could end this stalemate. Exhausted, the two sides finally agreed to pull back on November 1.

The Miike turmoil coincided with the 1960 struggle over the revision of the Japan-US Security Treaty and was seen by both labor and management not as a single workplace dispute but as a battle to the death between labor and capital, with other unions, other companies, and even the weight of government forces joining in. Yet the energy revolution meant that the outcome was preordained, and the struggle ended with the union humbled both financially and politically.

Distribution Revolution, Communications Revolution, What-Next Revolution

Energy was not the only field to experience changes so transformative as to warrant being called a revolution. Distribution, communication, transportation, and indeed all of the broadly defined service sectors that sustain our lives underwent equally sweeping changes.

The telephone is a good example. In 1955, there were approximately 2 million people and businesses with telephones. In 1970, a mere 15 years later, this number was 15 million. Many of these users, of course, were businesses, government offices, and the like. Looking just at home telephones, the number went from 180,000 in 1955 to 6.8 million in 1970, a 38-fold increase. On a per-household basis, this went from one in 100 households to one in 4 households having a telephone.

Distribution and retail also underwent major modernization, as typified by the advent of supermarkets. Even after Japan's rapid growth started, retail continued to be dominated by very small companies, mom-and-pop owner-operated stores, and legacy distributors. Like agriculture, it was a very traditional industry. Local merchants like the fishmonger and the greengrocer would come around to take orders and make deliveries. Women from the countryside would regularly come to town bearing big backpacks full of fresh-picked produce from their farming villages. And the tofu man would bicycle through the neighborhood blowing his distinctive horn—at which signal housewives would emerge with shallow pans into which he would ladle out cubes of tofu. Retail was a very different world from manufacturing with its cutting-edge machinery and other equipment. It was into this world that the supermarket intruded.

With its business model of narrow margins on a large variety of products, the supermarket was also distinguished by being self-service. It is widely believed that this self-service model was pioneered in Japan by Kinokuniya in the upscale Aoyama district of Tokyo in 1953; it was soon picked up by Daiei, Itō Yōkadō, and other big supermarket chains and was widespread by the late 1950s. The Japanese people readily took to the supermarket model, and supermarkets' share of the retail market has continued to increase over the years. Every five years, the government conducts a National Survey of Family Income and Expenditures. In 1964, it found that small retail shops accounted for 73 percent of sales and supermarkets 7.7 percent. When the rapid-growth era was over in 1974, these numbers were 63 percent and 19 percent. Twenty years later, in 1994, they were 41 percent and 29 percent. Fundamentally different from the steel industry's massive blast furnaces and LD furnaces that engendered major improvements in labor productivity, the supermarket was nonetheless a new business model and fully warrants Schumpeter's innovation label.

This was a time of innovation and revolution—the transportation revolution from trains to trucks, the energy revolution from coal to petroleum, the communications revolution, the distribution and retail revolution, and countless others too numerous to list. Engulfed in a bewildering array of radical changes, Japanese sometimes found it hard to keep up. Yet such was the rapid-growth era spawned by technological innovation.

CHAPTER 4

The Great Migration

New graduates from the countryside arrive at Ueno Station in Tokyo to take up the urban employment, 1962. (© Kyodo News)

Published in 1960, Namiki Masayoshi's *Nōson wa kawaru* (The Changing Rural Village) is an outstanding work clearly explaining the transformation that was taking place in Japanese agriculture and farm villages. As Namiki notes in his introduction:

> Looking just at what is going on with the next generation of farmers—the eldest sons who were expected to take over the family farms—over the last year or two, we see that over half of them have left farming and opted to work in other sectors as soon as they graduated from school. This is not an isolated phenomenon. Nearly a score of Japan's 47 prefectures have seen 70–80 percent of their natural-heir farmers leave agriculture for other work. True, the seeds of this transformation were sowed during the war, but it is only since the war's end—actually, only in the last four or five years—that it has become so pronounced. Of late, the depth, breadth, and speed of this transformation can best be described by likening it to an avalanche or a landslide. It has now become impossible for anyone or anything to stem this vast outflow.

This massive migration out of the farmlands that Namiki likened to an avalanche continued until the early 1970s, and Japan saw unprecedented internal migration throughout the rapid-growth period. Figure 5 hints at the impact this had on urban populations. Population movement into Japan's three largest urban areas increased sharply in the late 1950s and peaked just before the 1964 Tokyo Olympics, very much in step with the rapid-growth period. In the 1970s, as economic growth petered out, so did migration into the cities. Interestingly, the influx virtually came to an end in 1973–74, coinciding with the oil crisis of 1973. This coincidence has to be considered when discussing

Figure 5. Net population movement into and out of Japan's top three urban centers (Tokyo, Osaka, and Nagoya)

(thousand people)

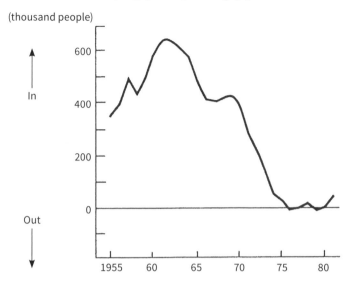

Based on data from the Annual Reports on Internal Migration in Japan Derived from the Basic Resident Registrations, published by the Statistics Bureau, Management and Coordination Agency.

the convergence of the end of the rapid-growth period and the oil crisis. While many people contend that the oil crisis marked the end of Japan's rapid growth, I disagree. However, that is an issue for the next chapter.

Trooping off to Work

It was primarily young people, especially new graduates taking their first jobs, who made up the vast bulk of this great migration. In 1950, prior to the economy's takeoff, two-thirds of girls and half of boys went to work immediately upon graduating from junior high school. In 1955, when rapid growth was taking off, the comparable figures were one in two for boys and girls. Even though these 15-year olds were still physically and intellectually immature in many ways, graduating from junior high meant going off to work. They were the first wave of the great migration from farm to city.

Table 10. Where junior high graduates went to work, 1961

	From								Total
	Hokkaido & Tōhoku	Kantō	Yamanashi & Nagano	Hokuriku	Kinki	Chūgoku	Shikoku	Kyūshū	
To Tokyo	16,269	11,218	1,921	3,103				1,857	38,713
	(42%)	(29%)	(5%)	(8%)				(5%)	
To Osaka				791	2,964	6,340	6,550	10,269	28,847
				(3%)	(10%)	(22%)	(23%)	(36%)	

Source: Ministry of Labor, Public Employment Security Statistics.
Notes: "Tokyo" here includes Kanagawa and Chiba prefectures. Only the top five source regions are shown for Tokyo and Osaka.

The employment statistics for 1961 show some 38 percent of the new junior-high graduates opted to go to work outside their native prefectures. Of these, 93 percent went to work in the Tokyo, Osaka, or Aichi (Nagoya) areas. For these people, going to work after junior high meant leaving their hometowns far behind. Table 10 shows the top five regions that supplied fresh-off-the-farm labor for enterprises in Tokyo and Osaka. As shown, a clear geographical division was at play: people from Hokkaido and Tōhoku going to Tokyo and people from Kyūshū, Shikoku, and Chūgoku going to Osaka. Japan is often said to be small, but there is a clear east-west divide even in this small country.

These people found jobs in the city through their local government employment agencies or their schools. Graduating in March, they then went off en masse in teacher-led groups to start their new lives. This was the famous *shūdan shūshoku* system. The national railway put on special trains for the occasion, and the point of arrival for the groups of young people coming into Tokyo from the north was Ueno Station. On April 26, 1959, the weekly *Shūkan Yomiuri* carried this report on the employment experiences of people from Aomori Prefecture's Yoshikawa Junior High School:

The special train for the new hires pulled into Ueno Station and was met, as always, by people from the Tokyo Labor Bureau and a number of people from Tokyo-area employment referral offices. Mr. Sudō led his flock of 30 young men and women to the nearby Shitaya Elementary School, where they were divided up into subgroups depending upon which part of Tokyo they were scheduled to go to work in and were then handed over to the care of the person who owned the shop where they would work.

Including new arrivals from other prefectures as well, there were more than a thousand people at the school, and Mr. Sudō had to raise his voice to say a few last words to his 30 students. "When you get to where you are going to work, be sure to work hard and do a good job. I am going to stop by in the next few days to make sure everything is okay and to see how you are doing. And then I will go back to Aomori."

Mr. Sudō spent the next two weeks going around to the different shops, but by the time he got to some of them, the former student he had come to see had already quit.

Some of the people in this group were accepted as blue-collar workers at major companies. Typically the young women worked in the textile industry or transistor factories. And some of the young men were taken on as apprentices, given three years of training, and then worked as journeymen. As noted in the previous chapter, these full-time regular employees who had graduated from junior high were considered the blue-collar elite and treated much better than the far more numerous ordinary hourly workers. Yet it was a decided minority that landed these preferential-status jobs at big companies. Far more common was to go to work for second- or third-tier companies where, despite being acclaimed as the "golden eggs" (*kin no tamago*) of the company's future, they spent their days frustrated at having to work and live marginal existences on the city's fringes.

An article in the April 26, 1959, weekly *Shūkan Myōjō* chronicled the not-atypical life of a young man named Koyama who came to Tokyo from Gunma Prefecture as part of a group and got a job at a name firm in Kōtō Ward:

His day starts at 6:00 a.m. He has until 7:00 to eat breakfast, wash the dishes, and get to his workstation. The people one year senior to him are responsible for the cooking.

The dining room has a bare wooden floor and is attached to the company president's house. There is a long unpainted wooden table where they eat. Breakfast is a miso broth soup with some greens in it, and the same greens are also provided salted to eat with the rice; lunch is some pickled radish and *tsukudani* with rice; and supper is just some pickled vegetables and rice. In the two weeks Koyama has been there, they have only had fish maybe three times. But it is not the absence of protein that bothers them. They have all come from the country where they grew their own rice, and it is hard not to gag at the stench of the big bowls of imported rice they get.

Work starts at 7:00, right after breakfast. Technically, it starts at 8:00, but everyone is expected to put in an hour off the clock and unpaid before that.

The lunch break runs from 12:15 to 1:00. This seems reasonable, but there is only one toilet for all 180 men, which is a real problem. There is inevitably a long wait to use the toilet, but the foreman screams at them if they are just standing and waiting. And very often the long waits result in the men getting gastrointestinal pains.

Supper is from 7:00 to 8:00. That is the end of the formal workday, but there is usually two hours of overtime after dinner. After that, they have time to themselves until it is lights-out around midnight. For the first week or so, they act like they are on a school excursion to some historical site, but the novelty soon wears off and the most-heard phrase is "I want to go home."

While there were some young men and women who decided this was not what they wanted and returned to their villages, most stayed in the city and simply shifted to different jobs. In either case, this was a far cry from the later-vaunted "lifetime employment" system. Although it only covers enterprises with 10 or more employees, Table 11's data are indicative of the way these new hires fresh out of junior high school changed jobs. The "new hires" and "percentage leaving" in this table are for students graduating junior high in both March 1963 and March 1964. Thus the numbers could possibly include some who were new hires in March 1963, quit their first jobs, and were new hires again between January and June 1964. This data problem aside, the numbers are nonetheless trend-indicative and it is worth using them to calculate the percentage of new hires who quit within the year.

As expected, the dropout rate was much higher for smaller enterprises than it was for companies with 500 or more employees. At enterprises with

Table 11. Junior high new hires leaving their employers within the year

Total number of employees at firm	New hires	Number leaving	Percentage leaving
10–29	57,500	10,000	17.4
30–99	114,200	20,500	18.0
100–499	155,400	20,900	13.4
500 and up	124,700	10,800	8.7
Total	451,800	62,200	13.7

Source: Ministry of Labor, Survey on Employment Trends, 1964.

10–99 employees, over one in six young men and women quit within six months of being hired. Extrapolating this out to a two-year span (four half-years), employee turnover averaged about 50 percent. As noted earlier, these data only cover enterprises with 10 or more employees, even though many junior-high graduates went to work at even smaller enterprises, typically family businesses. These were the people who went door-to-door for the greengrocer and the fishmonger, the people who rode their bicycles through crowded commercial districts balancing stacks of soba for delivery, and other young people who interacted with customers while the boss minded the store. Turnover was even higher at these establishments. If we assume turnover was not one in six but one in four, this would mean a rate of seven out of ten over a two-year period—with two of the seven changing jobs twice during the first two years.

Compiled by Iwamoto Jun, Figure 6 shows what happened over the next 10 years to the 35 young men and women who graduated from Miyagi Prefecture's Kaminuma Junior High School in the spring of 1963 and migrated together to Tokyo to start working. Overall, the pattern is much the same as that derived from the labor mobility data: there was still a very fluid labor market totally divorced from the idea of lifetime employment.

Figure 6. New hires from Kaminuma Junior High School (Miyagi Prefecture)

(1) Males

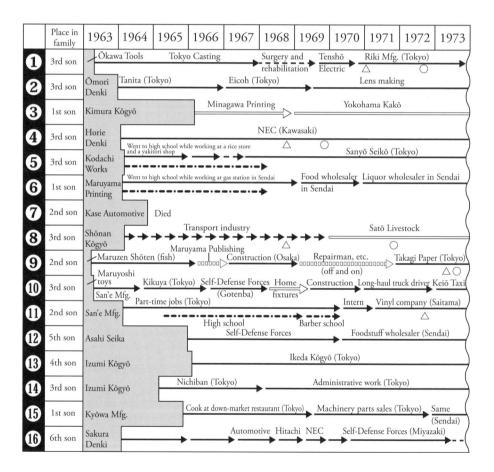

(2) Females

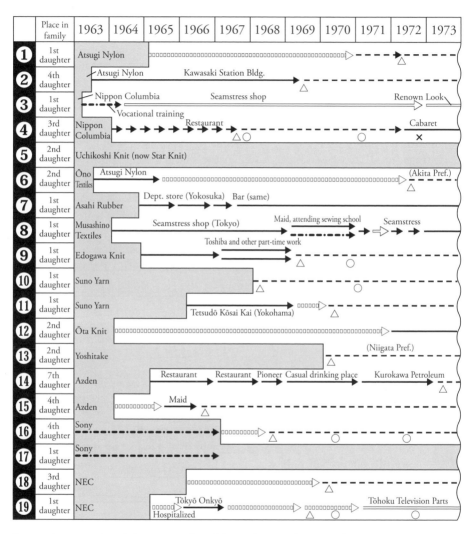

Source: Iwamoto Jun, "The New Junior High Graduates Who Arrived in Ueno 10 Years Ago: The Outcome of One Class's Employment," *Shūkan Shinchō*, June 21, 1973.

Changes in the Labor Market

Because working conditions such as pay were better in the city than in the countryside, the vast bulk of the young men and women who moved to the cities to work, regardless of whether they went as part of a group or individually, ended up staying there. In 1955, after the rapid-growth era started, the average wage in the lowest-wage prefecture was less than 40 percent of the figures for Tokyo and Osaka. Given the importance of this wage differential, it is worth looking at Table 12 and its data on wages for new employees in the different regions. Even though the disparities were small at the new-hire stage, a number of poorer-paid regions (Tōhoku, Kyūshū, and Shikoku) showed an average wage for new hires in 1960 of only about 70 percent of wages in Tokyo and Osaka. Even in the better-paid Hokkaido, San'yō, and Kita-Kantō regions, the starting wage was only about 80 percent of that in Tokyo and Osaka. These wage differentials were one factor driving labor mobility. Instead of joining the ranks of the country's farmers, young men and women moved from farms to cities to work as salaried employees. By 1959, more than half of the employed population were on salaries.

An article in the daily *Yomiuri Shimbun* on September 11, 1994, reported the reaction of one farming couple on seeing the pay envelope that their son brought home from his new job:

> "So this is your salary. And you'll keep getting it every month from now on, right? Lucky you!" The parents of 18-year-old Maekawa Minoru (now 53) stared at the plain manila envelope that he showed them back at their farm in April 1959.
>
> Inside the envelope was his 8,100 yen pay for 25 days' work—324 yen/day—and an accounting slip for the month. Maekawa was a Kintetsu Railway employee, a salaryman who had just received his first month's salary. Not only was it his first salary, it was his family's first exposure to the salary concept.

With the salary differential so significant, the question naturally arises: Why were urban wages so much higher than rural wages? One answer is that the urban workers' cost of living was higher, but that is not the whole story. A more basic reason is that productivity was higher in the manufacturing industries clustered around the cities than it was in farming. This higher productivity was sustained in large part by strong technological innovation

Table 12. Regional differences in starting salaries for new junior high graduates (Tokyo = 100)

	Hokkaido	Tōhoku	Kita-Kantō	Tokyo	Tōkai	Keihanshin (Kyoto, Osaka, and Kobe)	San'in	San'yō	Shikoku	Kita-Kyūshū	Minami-Kyūshū
1960	80	71	78	100	90	100	73	79	72	68	69
1964	83	75	89	100	93	98	83	89	80	79	72
1967	84	79	94	100	98	99	88	97	95	85	78

Source: Ministry of Labor, Survey of Starting Wages for New Graduates.

and capital investment, with conditions in the countryside not amenable to the same kind of productivity-enhancing innovation and investment. This is really what accounts for the wage disparities shown in Table 12. And it is these wage disparities that account for the fact that labor migrated from farms to cities throughout the rapid-growth years.

One more reason wages were lower in the rural areas is that there was a major population surplus in the rural areas for much of the first half of the rapid-growth era. This population surplus, variously termed excess labor and latent unemployment, was especially pronounced until 1961–62. There were already more corporate job openings than there were fresh junior-high graduates by the late 1950s, yet for other workers there were two or three job seekers for every job opening. Looking at this labor surplus in the context of the total labor market including new graduates, the surplus was essentially gone by 1961–62, when people in business, government, the media, and everywhere else switched to talking about the labor shortage.

Hitotsubashi University Professor Minami Ryōshin has referred to this shift in the structure of the labor market as a turning point for the Japanese economy. This "turning point" concept was first elucidated by Sir Arthur Lewis, who won the 1979 Nobel Prize in Economics for his outstanding analytical work on economic development. In order to analyze how a country develops, Lewis constructed a dual-sector model juxtaposing modern manufacturing against agriculture and other traditional (premodern) industries. In this model, the manufacturing sector that drives modernization benefits from being able to offer low wages because of the labor surplus in the agricultural

Table 13. Ratio of job seekers to job openings

	New junior high graduates	Others	Total
1955	0.91	4.6	3.6
1956	1.0	3.0	2.6
1957	0.83	2.5	2.1
1958	0.83	3.1	2.6
1959	0.83	2.3	2.0
1960	0.53	1.7	1.4
1961	0.37	1.3	1.0
1962	0.34	1.5	1.0
1963	0.38	1.4	0.6
1964	0.28	1.3	0.6
1965	0.27	1.6	0.6
1966	0.34	1.4	0.7
1967	0.29	1.0	0.4

Source: Ministry of Labor, Report on Employment Service.

sector. Yet as labor moves from agriculture to manufacturing, this labor surplus diminishes to zero. Lewis terms the juncture at which this happens the turning point. Drawing upon both theoretical considerations and empirical analysis, Minami concludes that the turning point for the Japanese economy was in the very early 1960s. This accords with the impression I get from the raw data in Table 13. The labor surplus was a thing of the past by the early 1960s, and the labor market most certainly grew gradually tighter in the latter half of the decade. This is also substantiated by the regional wage disparities in 1967, which, aside from some disparity for Tōhoku, Hokkaido, and Kyūshū, were much less than they had been in 1960.

Mirroring this transformation in the labor market, Japan's pattern of economic development underwent a major shift in the late 1960s, as illustrated in Figure 7 on the changing picture of regular employment in manufacturing. From the late 1950s to the early 1960s, the regular employment index rose 10 percent per year on average, yet this growth essentially stopped in 1964, the year the Olympic Games were held in Tokyo. And there was very little growth over the following 30 years.

This was not the result of manufacturing's having stopped expanding in the late 1960s. Indeed, manufacturing output basically doubled overall from

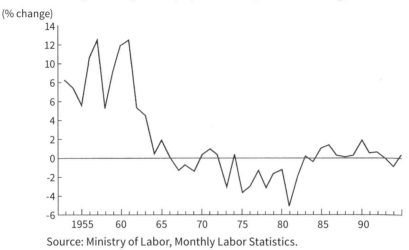

Figure 7. Regular employment index (in manufacturing)

(% change)

Source: Ministry of Labor, Monthly Labor Statistics.

1965 to 1970. This represented average annual growth of over 14 percent. The Izanagi Boom, which ran for 57 months from November 1965 through July 1970, was the longest period of sustained growth Japan had ever experienced. (This record stood until the first decade of the twenty-first century, when it was surpassed in duration by the anemic economic expansion that limped along for 69 months from January 2002 through October 2007.) Yet manufacturing employment did not expand in tandem with manufacturing output. As already mentioned, the labor market tightened, it was harder to hire new people, and industry shifted to investing heavily in labor-saving equipment starting around 1965. We have already discussed how innovation produced productivity-enhancing equipment that attracted new investment, but it should be noted that this innovation did not just yield greater production and better products but also induced strong investment in labor-saving machinery—equipment expressly intended to require less labor input. By the late 1960s, such investment had already achieved striking advances to put Japanese productivity on a par with the global leaders in steel, general machinery, electrical equipment, and a wide range of other industries.

Although the trend of increasing employment in the manufacturing sector flattened out, that does not mean the influx of labor from rural areas stopped.

Table 14. International comparison of productivity improvement by sector

(1) Average annual increase, 1960–64 (%)

Rank	Japan Sector	Average Increase	USA Sector	Average Increase	West Germany Sector	Average Increase	UK Sector	Average Increase
	All manu-facturing	30.1	All manu-facturing	23.7	All manu-facturing	17.4	All manu-facturing	17.3
1	Fossil fuels	89.0	Chemicals	34.8	Ceramics, stone & clay	41.8	Chemicals	35.6
2	Trans-portation equipment	73.2	Fossil fuels	34.1	Shipbuilding	35.3	Trans-portation equipment	24.3
3	Chemicals	45.1	Primary metals	29.3	Textiles	31.2	Quarry products	22.4
4	Iron & steel	37.8	Textiles	28.2	Wood & paper goods	29.6	Textiles	18.9
5	Precision machinery	37.1	Electrical equipment	25.8	Chemicals	20.0	Wood & lumber	17.3
6	Electrical equipment	33.6	Rubber & plastics	24.7	Foodstuffs	15.0	Textile products	17.0
7	Rubber products	31.0	Trans-portation equipment	24.3	Textile products	14.9	Foodstuffs	14.85
8	Paper & pulp	29.6	Paper & products	23.6	Nonferrous metals	10.0	Paper & printed goods	14.5
9	Textiles	28.4	Metal products	22.5	Iron & steel	7.0	Electrical equipment	13.7
10	General machinery	27.0	Wood & lumber	20.7	Trans-portation equipment	5.5	Leather & leather goods	13.0
11	Nonferrous metals	25.7	Nonmetallic mineral products	19.3	General machinery	4.6	Shipbuild-ing	10.5
12	Textile products	20.5	Foodstuffs	18.0	Electrical equipment	2.9	Primary metals	7.8
13	Ceramics, stone & clay	20.1	Textile products	17.8			Metal products	6.9
14	Metal products	11.9	Leather & leather goods	11.1				
15	Foodstuffs	0.3						

(2) Average annual increase, 1965–69 (%)

Rank	Japan Sector	Average Increase	USA Sector	Average Increase	West Germany Sector	Average Increase	UK Sector	Average Increase
	All manu-facturing	89.0	All manu-facturing	7.9	All manu-facturing	25.6	All manu-facturing	14.6
1	General machinery	168.4	Chemicals	21.6	Chemicals	58.9	Chemicals	46.7
2	Iron & steel	123.3	Foodstuffs	17.5	Electrical equipment	39.2	Textiles	31.9
3	Electrical equipment	119.7	Fossil fuels	15.2	Iron & steel	37.5	General machinery	25.5
4	Metal products	108.7	Paper & paper products	10.2	Wood & papers	33.5	Ceramics, stone & clay	12.5
5	Chemicals	91.7	Metal products	9.4	Textiles	29.2	Foodstuffs	8.8
6	Nonferrous metals	88.9	Nonmetallic mineral products	8.7	Nonferrous metals	25.3	Textile products	7.3
7	Paper & pulp	86.3	Rubber & plastics	7.4	Foodstuffs	24.1	Paper & printed goods	5.6
8	Trans-portation equipment	85.4	Textiles	7.2	Trans-portation equipment	23.7	Trans-portation equipment	5.2
9	Precision machinery	80.6	Wood & wood products	6.5	Ceramics, stone & clay	22.0	Primary metals	3.6
10	Textiles	76.2	General machinery	0.0	General machinery	20.3	Leather & leather goods	0.8
11	Rubber products	66.3	Textile products	-2.2	Shipbuild-ing	15.9	Wood & wood products	0.5
12	Fossil fuels	58.6	Primary metals	-3.1	Textile products	11.4	Shipbuild-ing	-0.8
13	Ceramics, stone & clay	56.8	Trans-portation equipment	-4.0			Metal products	-9.3
14	Foodstuffs	25.8	Leather & leather goods	-4.8				
15	Textile products	11.8						

Source: Economic Planning Agency, Economic White Paper, 1973.
Note: Labor productivity was derived by dividing production by labor employed.

As shown in Table 15, some 800,000 people, including about 500,000 new graduates, moved from agriculture to nonagricultural sectors year after year in the latter 1960s. Yet unlike in earlier times, they were absorbed not by manufacturing but by distribution (both wholesale and retail), services, construction, and other nonmanufacturing sectors.

Looking at Table 15, we see that the percentage of new graduates leaving their rural villages declined over the period in question. This reflects the fact that a considerable number of people who left farming did not migrate to the big cities but rather found nonfarming employment closer to home. Still living in their rural villages but commuting to nonfarming jobs nearby, such people came to be the mainstream in the 1970s and later. As a corollary, the inflow into the big three urban areas (Tokyo, Osaka, and Nagoya) started slowing around the mid-1960s—but did not stop, as evidenced by the some 400,000–500,000 people who moved to the big cities every year. Even as the pattern of Japanese labor mobility shifted in the late 1960s, the economy definitely stayed on the rapid-growth track.

Table 15. Labor movement from agricultural to nonagricultural sectors

	Total (x10,000 people)	New graduates from farm families (x10,000 people)	Total percentage leaving villages
1958	51	—	71.9
1959	62	31	63.2
1960	69	32	59.0
1961	75	33	56.9
1962	86	48	54.0
1963	93	54	47.0
1964	89	51	46.6
1965	85	56	48.2
1966	81	56	46.9
1967	82	57	45.1
1968	79	54	43.0
1969	80	51	41.3

Source: Ministry of Agriculture and Forestry, Census of Agriculture and Forestry.
Note: Figures do not include people leaving their villages to work elsewhere on a temporary basis.

Increasing Numbers of Households

As more and more people moved from rural villages to the big cities and suburbs, there was inevitably an increase in the number of new households in those areas. In 1950, right before the rapid-growth era started, the rural villages where half of the Japanese population lived were typically composed of three-generation households. But when people moved to the city, they started out as single-individual households and only later graduated to married-couple households and then married-couple-plus-children households. Overall, this was a shift from extended families to nuclear families.

Figure 8 shows the increase in households during the rapid-growth era. Population growth is one of the perennial issues in any discussion of economic growth, and the figure shows that this key index held steady at about one percent throughout the rapid-growth period (the spike in 1970 attributable to the inclusion of Okinawa in the national census in light of its imminent reversion to Japan). Although not shown here, the number of working-age people (the labor population) also grew on average 1–2 percent per year during this period, with no major drop-off in the 1970s and after. Along

Figure 8. Rates of change in number of households and population

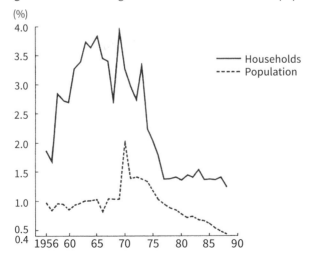

Note: Okinawa is included in figures for 1970 and later.

with this population growth, the number of households also rose during the period, twin-peaking at around 4 percent growth with the influx into the big cities. Yet the rate of increase in the number of households fell sharply in the 1970s, leveling off at about 1.5 growth percent from 1975 to 1990. From this, it is apparent that the increase in the number of households and economic growth correlate more closely than population growth and economic growth.

This then raises the question of why the increase in household numbers and economic growth correlate so closely. The most obvious answer is that people moving to urban areas to work needed to establish new households, as already explained. The link that joins the establishment of new households and economic growth is demand creation. If everyone in rural areas is living in a three-generation household, they only need one washing machine, one refrigerator, and one of almost everything else. But if someone from the three-generation household moves to the city and establishes a new household, that household also needs a washing machine, a refrigerator, and one of all the other household appliances that sold especially well in the cities and drove much of the economic growth—plus the additional electricity to power them. The exodus of young people from farm to city thus did much to create and sustain demand for consumer durables.

This growth in demand for consumer durables in turn generated additional upstream demand for high-quality steel, petrochemical products, and more. In this way, the increase in the number of households had far-reaching ramifications going well beyond consumer durables and prompting investment in a wide range of industries—which then translated into additional economic growth as investment begat investment. It is easy to track this investment both upstream and downstream, but it should be remembered that it was basically grounded in population mobility and the increase in the number of households. In a sense, population mobility and the increase in household numbers were the ultimate causes of Japan's economic growth. Yet both numbers fell off sharply in the early 1970s, cutting the ground out from under the economy's expansion.

Overcrowded Cities, Underpopulated Villages

As young men and women moved from their rural villages to take jobs in the big cities, another problem arose: the cities became overcrowded and the villages underpopulated. Similarly, because most of the big industrial parks and developments were in and around Tokyo, Osaka, and Nagoya, all of which are on the Pacific coast, a population imbalance arose between the Pacific side of the country and the Sea of Japan side. Although the terms have fallen out of use, the Pacific side was often called Japan's face and the Sea of Japan side Japan's backside. The sociologist Tominaga Ken'ichi has suggested that the Pacific coast urban population ranking trends reverse-mirror population ranking trends on the Sea of Japan side.

This was not peculiar to the postwar era but was a continuation, albeit a conspicuous example, of the population movement that accompanied industrialization starting in the Meiji era (1868–1912).

Looking at just a few examples for 1878, 1920, and 1985, Kanazawa dropped from 5 to 11 to 31; Niigata from 17 to 19 to 24; and Tottori from 18 to 77 to 141. These are all on the Sea of Japan side. Tokyo and Osaka on the Pacific side stayed at in first and second place.

In the Edo era, most castle towns throughout Japan were pretty much the same size, the exceptions being Edo (where the Tokugawa government was located), Osaka (which was the prime commercial center), and Kyoto (the titular capital where the emperor resided). The primary industry being agriculture, there was no particular advantage to be gained from the population concentrations that industrialization demands. Quite the contrary, agriculture being land-intensive, it was advantageous to have the population spread out. But manufacturing, for which the main factors of production are capital (for tools and equipment) and labor, was concentrated in relatively small areas throughout the land. Kita-Kyūshū and other cities that had grown up in the

Table 16. Population rankings of select cities

		1878	1920	1985
Sea of Japan side	Kanazawa	5	11	31
	Toyama	9	35	55
	Fukui	15	37	80
	Matsue	16	63	140
	Niigata	17	19	24
	Tottori	18	77	141
Tōhoku	Hirosaki	19	73	115
	Morioka	26	53	90
	Yonezawa	29	52	218
Pacific side	Wakayama	7	23	39

Meiji years (Tokyo, Osaka, and Nagoya) were firmly established as commercial centers by the start of the rapid-growth era. Then, with the quantum leap in manufacturing and industrialization during the rapid-growth years, these industrial sites served as population magnets.

Looking at Tokyo, for example, the February 1944 population of 7,270,000 was down to less than half (3,490,000) in November 1945 as a result of the firebombings, evacuations, and other wartime causes. Yet it rebounded to 6,280,000 by 1950, before the start of the rapid-growth period, and stood at close to double that (11,410,000) when the rapid-growth era ended in 1970. This population growth included both natural increases (births minus deaths) and increases due to net inflows into Tokyo from elsewhere.

In Tokyo's case, the net inflows from other prefectures nosedived in the early 1960s and turned negative in the second half of the decade. In this respect, Tokyo was five years ahead of the other two major urban centers (Osaka and Nagoya) shown in Figure 5. The two main reasons for this reversal—and they are related—were the sharp rise in Tokyo real estate prices and the near impossibility for new arrivals to find a place to live. Thus the people moving to the Tokyo area did not move to Tokyo proper but rather settled in neighboring prefectures, notably Kanagawa, Saitama, and Chiba.

Yet the fact that people chose to live in the suburbs rather than the urban center did not resolve the underlying problem. Instead, it created new problems, such as the crowded trains during rush hours when people commuted to and from work. Although it is not known when the rail lines hired their first body-pushers to squeeze more passengers into the commuter trains, Tokyo was already promoting off-hour commutes as early as 1961 to alleviate what was termed "the commuter hell." At the same time, the inadequacy of Tokyo's capital infrastructure investment occasionally resulted in summertime water outages.

As mentioned earlier, the flip side of this overpopulation in the cities was that the rural villages became largely deserted. So extreme was this depopulation that, in the space of a mere 20 years, rural villages and the rural village culture that had been built up over the previous two millennia were pushed to the brink of extinction. The single decade from 1960 to 1970 saw the number of rural households decline by about 700,000 and agriculture's share of the total working population declined from 29 percent to just 16 percent. This was an astounding drop, especially when you consider that about half of Japan's total workforce was engaged in agriculture in 1950. With these

Table 17. Tokyo's population growth, 1950–70

	Net population growth (thousands)			Net growth rate (%)			Shares of total net growth (%)	
	Natural increase	Net inflow	Total	Natural increase	Net inflow	Total	Natural increase	Net inflow
1950–55	44	132	176	6.9	21.1	28.1	24.8	75.2
1956–60	48	117	165	6.0	14.5	20.5	29.2	70.8
1961–65	68	51	119	7.0	5.2	12.2	57.4	42.7
1966–70	83	-29	54	7.6	-2.6	5.0	153.1	-53.1

Source: *Tōkyō hyakunenshi* (100-Year History of Tokyo), vol. 6, 1972.

Table 18. Population density, 1955–75
(people per km²)

	1955	1965	1975
Tokyo	3,973	5,357	5,441
Osaka	2,552	3,618	4,455
Kanagawa	1,236	1,866	2,676
Aichi	745	948	1,158
Saitama	595	793	1,269
Kagoshima	224	203	188
Shimane	140	124	116
Kōchi	124	114	114
Akita	116	110	106
Iwate	93	92	91

Source: Population Census.

changes, agriculture's share of GNP also slipped, from 20 percent in 1955 to only 7 percent in 1970. By the time the rapid growth ended, agriculture was no longer the mainstay of the economy.

Nor was that all. At the same time as the farming population declined, the bulk of the remaining farmers and farm families stopped farming full-time and worked part-time in some of the many nonagricultural jobs that rapid economic growth had opened up. Other scholars have already covered the shift to agriculture as a part-time pursuit, so there is no need to go into it in any depth here, but it is still worth noting that half of all farmers in 1970 earned the bulk of their income from nonagricultural employment and saw agriculture as a source of supplemental income. Only 15 percent of farmers were full-time farmers. Working-age farm children also sought jobs off the farm, leaving the actual farming to the three *chans*—*jii-chan* (grandpa), *baa-chan* (grandma), and *kaa-chan* (mom). Significantly, the part-time farmers who earned the bulk of their income from nonfarm pursuits enjoyed incomes higher than those of full-time farmers. It is especially noteworthy here that this shift away from full-time farming was particularly prevalent among farmers who grew rice, which was Japan's staple crop and whose cultivation had long been regarded as more a mission than a job. The long process of rapid growth did not just diminish agriculture's importance, it resulted in considerable hollowing out of the agricultural sector.

The basic law on agriculture drafted by the Ikeda (Hayato) administration in 1961 envisioned a future for Japanese agriculture in which the exodus of people from the rural villages and the dwindling number of farming families would lead to each family's farming a broader expanse of land, which would in turn lend itself to mechanization and productivity improvements. However, the reality was that the changes led to a rise in the number of part-time farmers and the spread of three-*chan* agriculture. In addition, government regulations were used to enforce mandatory production curtailments when rice production exceeded demand. Under this system, starting in 1971, farm families were paid 30,000 yen per 1,000 square meters for *not* producing rice—for doing nothing. As agrarian economist Saeki Naomi explained it, this resulted in large numbers of farmers getting paid for not farming, meaning that they were making their living simply by letting their land lie fallow. The rapid-growth policies transformed Japan's human landscape by encouraging large numbers of people to move off the farms and to the cities. And in the process, it precipitated the collapse of Japanese farming as it had existed since prehistoric times.

CHAPTER 5

The Mechanism of Rapid Growth

Counting out bonuses for department store employees, 1966. (© Kyodo News)

The flowcharts in Figure 9 provide a rough depiction of the self-sustaining mechanism by which Japan achieved the rapid growth that produced its revolutionary transformation in less than two decades. As seen, this is an interlocking and mutually reinforcing mechanism in which each element is both a cause and an effect—is both the result of other forces and itself a force acting upon other elements, such that the whole results in accelerated growth.

Before Rapid Growth

Underlying Japan's rapid growth was the people's ardent desire to modernize their lifestyles—which meant a consuming drive to Americanize their lives and catch up with the United States. Drawing upon this latent demand, companies embarked upon technological innovation and the capital investment needed to incorporate the new technologies into their production facilities. While capital investment (corporate investment in plant and equipment) is sometimes referred to as the strategic variable and the key to Japan's rapid growth, it would be wrong to assume this capital investment started as soon as World War II ended. The Japanese economy was completely devastated by the war, and it was not until the Korean War (1950–53) and its accompanying procurement orders that industry was able to embark upon its initial burst of investment. We must never forget that this blessing for the Japanese economy was a tragedy for our neighbors next door.

The American forces that occupied Japan after the war ended in August 1945 initially imposed policies that were very harsh and punitive. The thinking was that postwar Japan's standard of living should not be any better than that of the countries Japan had occupied during the war, so the basic policy of the occupying authorities was to restrict Japanese manufacturing to textiles

Figure 9. The circulatory mechanism of rapid growth

(1) Within Japan

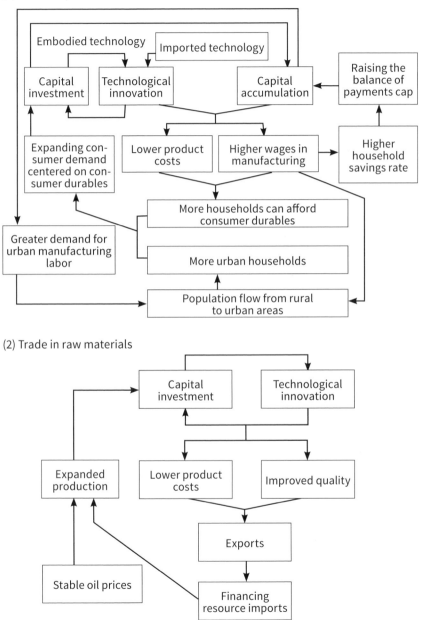

(2) Trade in raw materials

and other light industry. In December 1945, plans were announced to transfer over 2.5 million tons of steelmaking capacity—equivalent to about one-fourth of the prewar production capacity—to the Philippines. While this plan was later abandoned, it is indicative of how Occupation thinking sought to quash Japanese investment in plant and equipment. Even though there was pent-up demand for lifestyle modernization and hence for upgrading production facilities, there was no way this could be translated into robust capital investment given conditions at the time.

The turnabout in Occupation policy took place in 1948 with the outbreak of the Cold War, when irreconcilable differences emerged between the Soviet Union and the other Allied countries it had fought alongside in World War II. Along with embarking upon its ambitious Marshall Plan to get the countries of Western Europe back on their economic feet, the United States fundamentally rethought Japan's position in the Far East and pivoted from preaching demilitarization and economic restrictions to advocating that Japan be a bulwark against Communism. This entailed prioritizing the rebuilding of Japan's economy, including the full array of heavy industry. Symbolic of this change in Occupation policy was the approval granted for the import of heavy oil for steel production. The policy shift was formally recognized in the April 1948 "Report on the Economic Position and Prospects of Japan and Korea and the Measures Required to Improve Them" (Johnston Report).

The next year, Joseph Dodge, who was president of the Detroit Bank, was dispatched to Japan by President Harry Truman to advise on how to rebuild the Japanese economy. The exchange rate was set at 360 yen to the dollar. Dodge pursued a harsh austerity policy, which came to be called the Dodge Line, to quell inflation, but this threw the economy into a severe recession. For example, Toyota Motors, one of Japan's leading industrial concerns today, was forced to the brink of bankruptcy, and the conditionalities for its bailout forced it to split itself into two companies (automotive production and sales) and carry out sweeping personnel reductions that provoked near-fatal labor strife. The fact that even Toyota was pushed to the brink is indicative of how deep the Dodge Line recession was. Yet just when Japan was feeling the full brunt of this recession, the Korean War broke out, sparking Japan's first postwar capital investment boom. A few years later, the country was on the road to rapid growth.

Looking back on the events that preceded rapid growth, it is clear that international developments such as the Cold War had a tremendous impact on Japan's postwar recovery. This recovery would, of course, not have been possible without the creative ingenuity and hard work of the Japanese people, but the global circumstances were so very crucial that I sometimes wonder if Japan was not just a pawn that lucked out, got plopped down on the eighth rank, and found itself made a queen.

The Causes and Effects of Rapid Growth

Although Japanese companies were more than fully aware of the need to modernize their equipment and import new technology, they were unable to actually do this until the procurement boom sparked by the Korean War. It was only in 1951 that the steel industry's first round of rationalization and modernization got underway with the upgrading of rolling mills and the expansion of open-hearth furnaces. This was also the year Toray signed its nylon technology licensing agreement with DuPont.

Technological innovation encouraged investment in new plants and equipment, which then enabled companies to achieve economies of scale, both reducing production costs and improving product quality. This ambitious investment in steel and other upstream industries then made it possible for a wide range of downstream industries to achieve cost reductions and quality enhancements as well. Typical examples were such downstream consumer durables as washing machines and television sets, where costs and hence prices could be slashed sufficiently to put products within reach of the vast latent demand.

We saw earlier that this combination of technological innovation and capital investment improved labor productivity and ended up raising wages and income. When prices went down and incomes went up, the result was an almost wildfire-like diffusion of consumer durables. And because this frenzied rush to buy consumer durables generated additional demand for high-grade metals and plastics, it induced additional innovation and investment in these material industries. This is just one example of the self-reinforcing cycles that were at work.

In another example, the higher wages that were paid to workers in the more productive urban manufacturing industries drew rural residents, especially young people, to the cities, with the collateral result that there was a sharp rise in the number of people living alone or in nuclear families. The increase in the number of households was undoubtedly one result of Japan's rapid growth, but it was also a driving factor in creating increased demand for all manner of goods and services. As these young people left their extended-family households in the countryside and set up new households in the city, they inevitably generated new demand for consumer durables, electricity, and more. The movement from farm to city and the consequent increase in the number of households were simultaneously the results of economic growth and the causes of greater economic growth. This is the circular operation of the rapid-growth mechanism as depicted in the top half of Figure 9.

How were wage hikes and expanded capital investment compatible? Wage-paying companies having to finance the capital investment that was the key to growth, one might reasonably expect they would have held wages and other costs down to free up funds for this investment—one might think of wage hikes as detrimental to investment. This line of thought finds voice in the argument that low wages are important for international competitiveness, the underlying premise being that wages are a growth-negative cost pulling money away from investment, pushing prices up, and eroding international competitiveness.

Admittedly, low wages were advantageous when Japanese growth was driven by exports, primarily of textiles, before the war. Yet Japan's postwar growth was essentially different from the prewar growth in being powered not by exports but by domestic demand, which meant wages were less of a factor.

There is obviously no point in investing to make products that you cannot sell, which is why companies only invest in making products that they think will sell well. What sold well during the rapid-growth years? Looking at both upstream and downstream industries, from raw materials to finished products, the things that sold best were such consumer durables as washing machines and television sets. As noted in Chapter 2, sales of such consumer durables took off after prices came down and incomes went up sufficiently to make them mass-affordable. Holding wages down was not the critical factor here. Rather, it was important that wages and income *not* be held down—that they be sufficiently high to support this sales growth.

This is not, of course, to say "the higher the better" for wages. But it is to argue that vigorous capital investment in line with market growth should result in improved productivity due to newer technologies being used and economies of scale being achieved—and that these productivity enhancements should then give companies the leeway to raise wages commensurately.

Unlike the prewar Japanese economy, which saw numerous bouts of wage stagnation, the rapid-growth economy saw higher wages as a definite plus factor for sustaining growth led by domestic demand.

The End of Rapid Growth

The rapid-growth era drew to a close around the beginning of the 1970s. As shown in Figure 10, the average real growth rate, which had been around 10 percent in the years 1955–72, fell to only about four percent a year in 1973–90. It is interesting in this context to compare Figure 5 on population mobility, Figure 8 on the numbers of new households, and Figure 10 on economic growth. The three trend lines move very much in concert. Also noticeable is that growth was roughly halved in the 1970s and beyond. Various terms have been coined to describe this period, such as the "stable-growth era," but whatever one calls it, it was definitely a time of slower growth.

What was it that brought the rapid growth to an end? This is an important question that reverberates even today. To answer it, we need to go back and

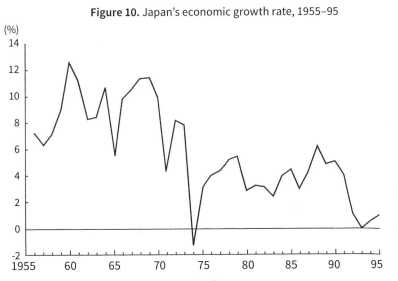

Figure 10. Japan's economic growth rate, 1955–95

Source: Economic Planning Agency, National Accounts.
Note: The graph shows the annual changes in gross domestic expenditures (essentially equivalent to GNP) in 1990 real values.

look at the actual mechanisms that facilitated rapid growth and the features that characterized the Japanese economy at the time. Looking just at the timing, many observers have identified the oil crisis of 1973–74 as the prime culprit responsible for killing Japan's rapid growth. While this has surface plausibility, it fails to be convincing on closer examination.

The oil crisis crashed onto the global economic scene in the autumn of 1973. In January 1973, a barrel of crude cost 2.60 US dollars. In January 1974, it was 11.70 US dollars. Prior to the oil crisis, Japanese inflation had already been running at an uncomfortably high rate due to extreme easy-money policies. The oil crisis further inflamed this condition, pushing inflation to levels unseen since the chaotic period just after World War II. People old enough to remember those times doubtless recall housewives' panicked buying and hoarding of toilet paper, prompted by fears that this and other essential commodities would disappear from store shelves.

The oil crisis posed an almost existential shock for the Japanese economy, which registered a growth rate of minus 1.2 percent in 1974—the first such negative figure since the war. The oil crisis also convinced large numbers of businesspeople, bureaucrats, politicians, economists, and others that rapid growth was a thing of the past. But even though it is easy to see how the spike in crude oil prices could temporarily depress GNP levels, it is very difficult to explain how sharply increasing oil prices could have a permanent depressive effect on the growth rate—not entirely impossible, but requiring a quite convoluted and intricate theoretical construction.

There are several reasons even the convoluted theoretical construct needed would be unconvincing. First is the impact of the second oil crisis. The global economy underwent a second oil crisis in 1979–80. The barrel of crude that cost 13.30 US dollars in January 1979 was 28 US dollars in June 1980. Yet Japan, which had turned in the worst performance of any industrial country in terms of both inflation and economic growth in the wake of the first oil crisis, was not that badly hurt by this second oil crisis. Indeed, looking at the decade following the second oil crisis, it may be said that the crisis had essentially zero influence on the average growth rate. If the spike in oil prices had really had that decisive an impact on Japan's economic growth rate during the first oil crisis, you would expect the average growth rate to have been even worse after the second oil crisis. It was not.

Some might counter that oil prices jumped fourfold during the first oil crisis but rose far less dramatically during the second crisis. Yet the rebuttal to this is to be found in the fact that these higher oil prices resulted in income transfers from Japan to the oil-exporting countries equivalent to 3.8 percent of GNP in the first crisis and 4.1 percent during the second crisis, meaning that the actual impact on the Japanese economy was roughly the same in both cases.

Another very interesting "but what about?" shows up when we look at the South Korean economy, Korea being right next door and also a major oil-importing nation like Japan. While it got off relatively lightly during the first oil crisis, its real GNP growth slipped into negative territory with the second oil crisis. Even though the same external factors were at play, Japan and South Korea showed very different outcomes in the two crises.

From these and other facts, it may be concluded that the argument that the oil crises—particularly the sudden jump in oil prices in 1973—were fundamentally responsible for snuffing out Japan's rapid economic growth is at best too simplistic. While it is true that the first oil crisis did have an effect on the Japanese economy, it did not bring about the end of the rapid-growth era but simply accelerated the shift in the industrial structure—a shift that was already underway in the early 1970s—from raw materials to finished machinery and equipment.

Given that the oil crisis does not seem to have been the primary reason the rapid-growth era drew to an end, what are the other possibilities? It is not that difficult to come up with a suspect if we look at the top of Figure 9 again. Here we see that Japan's rapid growth was driven by vigorous capital investment and grounded in robust sales of consumer durables, population urbanization, and an increase in the number of households. From this, it is clear that rapid economic growth would wind down once (1) the excess rural population had been absorbed by the urban industrial sector and both labor mobility and new household starts slowed and (2) the diffusion of consumer durables was largely complete and new capital investment could not be justified by any rational expectation of stronger market demand.

Such was the state of the economy in the very late 1960s. As indicated in Figure 3 earlier, additional demand for washing machines, television sets, and the other coveted consumer durables had largely peaked by the end of the 1960s. And as seen in Chapter 4, there was a sudden drop-off in population mobility in the early 1970s, well before the 1973 oil crisis. Additionally, the expansion of regular employment in manufacturing, which had been a major engine of growth, died out even earlier, in the late 1960s. Even though people were still leaving agriculture, they were increasingly commuting from their homes, substantially lowering the percentage of people who actually left their rural villages to live elsewhere. As a result, the rate of increase in the number of new households plateaued and then declined in the early 1970s.

Deprived of its underpinnings, there was no way or reason capital investment alone could continue to sustain economic growth. In company after company, investment peaked around 1970, well before the oil crisis. This is illustrated in stark relief by Table 5's data on investment in the petrochemical industry which, far from being an exception, was close to typical. It was these changes in the domestic situation that were the fundamental reasons for the winding down of the rapid-growth era. The oil crisis might have been growth's death knell, but it was by no means the underlying cause of death.

Another theory that has been advanced to explain the slowing of Japan's economic growth is that the importation of new technology dried up. True, foreign-developed technology was an important factor in Japan's postwar technological innovation and hence its postwar economic growth. LD steelmaking, nylon, and transistors were all invented overseas. Equally true, capital investment to catch up with Western technology levels—which had gotten way ahead of Japan's in the years from the mid-1930s to the late 1940s when Japanese research stood still—was an important factor sustaining the subsequent rapid growth. Thus the fact that the import of foreign technology largely dried up in the very late 1960s leads some people to contend that this was a basic cause accounting for the end of the rapid growth.

However, this "drying up of technology imports" explanation fails to convince. As seen earlier in Table 14, Japan had already achieved world-class or better productivity levels by the late 1960s in general machinery, electrical machinery, transport machinery, precision machinery, and throughout the broad-based machinery industry, as well as in steel, metal products, paper and pulp, and a broad range of other industries. Indeed, productivity growth rates were even better in the second half of the 1960s than in the first half. While technology imports may have accounted for much of the increased productivity in the 1950s and early 1960s, they cannot plausibly be credited with the productivity improvements in the latter part of the 1960s, which were far greater than the Western countries achieved. It would be more natural to attribute the pace-setting productivity gains that Japan achieved in this period to home-grown technological innovation.

In fact, productivity continued to improve in manufacturing as broadly defined, particularly in the machinery and metal products industries, even into the 1970s. Combined with the yen's depreciation (triggered by the oil crisis), this and robust corporate investment in technological innovation made Japan's machinery industry a world leader. While this was one cause of the abrasive trade friction with the United States and Western Europe in the 1980s, it had its roots in the technological revolution of the late 1960s. Putting all of this together, the idea that the drying up of technology imports was responsible for stalling Japan's economic growth is clearly unconvincing.

The High Household Savings Rate

What of the other explanations offered to elucidate why the growth died?

One other explanation that has been bandied about is the change in Japan's high household savings rate. Savings are essentially what you do not consume today but put aside for possible consumption tomorrow, and many identify this deferral of consumption as the key to rapid economic growth and non-deferral as responsible for the loss of growth momentum.

Of course, the Japanese household savings rate did not start off high. In the four years 1947–50, the savings rate for working households in Tokyo clocked in at 1.9 percent, minus 2.2 percent, 1.6 percent, and 1.5 percent. This was in the period shortly after the war, when many families had trouble putting food on the table and urban working people were lucky to break even, let alone save. Indeed, 1948's negative rate means that people were drawing down their meager savings. The only ones who were able to put money aside at the time were farmers and other sole proprietors.

Yet by the time economic growth got into full swing in 1955, Japan's household savings rate topped 10 percent, after which it largely tracked GDP growth, peaking in the mid-1970s. Households of employees drawing salaries were the mainstay of savings during the rapid-growth era. Such households accounted for more than half of the total by the early 1960s and were the primary beneficiaries of Japan's rapid growth. Raises and bonuses combined to push their earnings up at an astounding pace of over 10 percent a year. Moreover, these were not expected or promised hikes but were unexpected windfall injections of new income that they received year after year for over a decade. Earning more money than they thought they would, these are the people who sustained the savings rate. The high savings rate was not a cause but a result of the high economic growth rate.

That said, it must be admitted that this savings rate, high by international

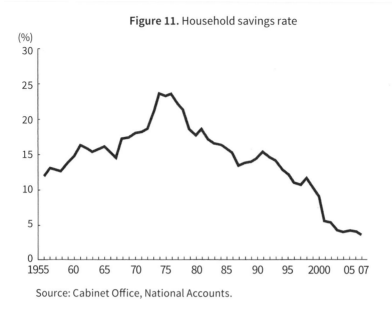

Figure 11. Household savings rate

Source: Cabinet Office, National Accounts.

standards, was a factor sustaining the growth rate. To see how this worked, it is important to understand that just putting excess money under the mattress does nothing to fuel the economy—because the real driver for economic growth is corporate capital investment.

What would happen if companies embarked upon robust capital investment while people, instead of saving, were spending all of their money buying this and that? Because corporate investment plus personal consumption equals total demand, it is very possible total demand would outstrip the nation's production capacity. This would then trigger inflation and make it impossible for corporations to finance their capital investment plans.

Even if that did not come to pass, the higher level of consumer goods production would put increased pressure on the parts and materials suppliers, which would in turn, in Japan's case, mean importing more. Before long, imports would exceed exports and, with the exchange rate fixed as it was, Japan would soon be eating into its foreign currency reserves (dollar savings). Because this would not be sustainable, the Bank of Japan would tighten the money supply, interest rates would rise, and capital investment would be curtailed. Economists often talk about the balance of payments ceiling, but what this really means, at least for a country without abundant natural resources of its own, is the constraint on how much natural resources its economic and export growth will allow it to import. All of the episodes of monetary tightening during the rapid-growth era were in response to the danger Japan would end up importing more than it could afford. Even countries with high growth rates inevitably run up against a balance of payments ceiling, but this happens sooner and with more modest investment increases if the household savings rate is low.

A higher household savings rate means a lower consumption rate and thus sustains rapid economic growth by freeing up resources for capital investment. Because capital investment was, as mentioned earlier, the lead player in Japan's economic growth, household savings, without which this investment would not have been possible, should be credited as an award-winning supporting actor on this stage.

Exports vs. Resource Import Costs

Looking specifically at the Japanese economy, exports are a perennial issue. But what role did exports play in the rapid growth story?

It has often been pointed out that the prewar Japanese economy was export-led. For approximately half a century, from the late nineteenth century to the 1930s, Japan's export volume grew 25-fold even as global trade overall grew only 2.5-fold. The prewar economy was strongly influenced by the ups and downs of exports, particularly after World War I. The very strong growth during World War I and the fact that the Japanese economy was able to continue to grow in the 1930s even as the Western economies were battered by the Great Depression can both be attributed to strong exports.

What of the period after World War II, which is our primary concern here? Benefiting from the relative undervaluation of the yen and the fixed exchange rate of 360 yen to the dollar from the time it was set in 1949 until the currency was floated in 1971, Japan was able to engineer dynamic growth by building upon strong exports of steel, ships, ammonium sulfate, cement, automobiles, electrical equipment, and almost every other industry producing exportable goods. Almost without fail, corporate management was united in promoting exports. Sony was no exception. As Sony co-founder Morita Akio wrote in his *Made in Japan*:

Although our company was still small and we saw Japan as a quite large and potentially active market, it was the consensus among Japanese industrialists that a Japanese company must export goods in order to survive. With no natural resources except our people's energy, Japan had no alternative. And so it was natural for us to look to foreign markets. Besides, as business prospered, it became obvious to me that if we did not set our sights on marketing abroad, we would not grow to be the kind of company Ibuka and I had envisioned. (*Made in Japan*, 74)

As explained below, however, management's focus on export promotion was not at odds with the idea of domestic-demand-led growth. Exports were important for the Japanese economy, but "important" does not mean that exports were the main driver of Japanese economic growth.

A number of methods are available to show that the postwar rapid growth was driven not by exports but by domestic demand. The simplest and most direct is to collect the data on consumption, capital investment, fiscal spending, net exports (exports minus imports), and the other categories and to look at how much, in percentage terms, the different categories contributed to overall growth. Doing this, we find that net exports contributed all of one percent to growth during the period 1955–72. Net exports are a decidedly minor factor in seeking to explain Japan's rapid growth. They were, however, a significant 13 percent contributor to sustaining the stable growth that Japan experienced in 1973–85 after the rapid-growth party ended. In the early 1980s, when the trade friction with the United States was at its height, net exports' contribution to Japanese economic growth was up to 38 percent.

Looking at shorter-cycle ups and downs, exports and domestic demand were very often pushing in opposite directions. Time after time, when domestic demand was booming, exports were down and acted as a brake on the economy, and when domestic demand was down, exports were strong and acted to sustain the economy. This was the standard pattern, but it was reversed during the stable-growth years.

While it is difficult to find any evidence that exports served directly to ramp up the economy during the rapid-growth years, it may well be that exports worked indirectly to stimulate capital investment, which was the main driver of growth. Yet even here, closer examination reveals that exports had their main impact after rapid growth had already ended in 1970. The automotive industry is recognized as being one of Japan's manufacturing mainstays, and

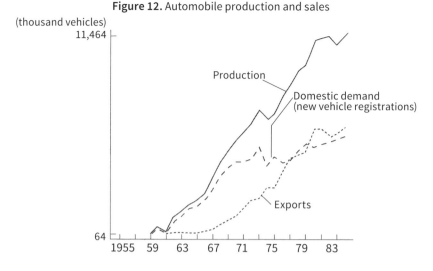

Figure 12. Automobile production and sales

(thousand vehicles)

11,464

Production

Domestic demand
(new vehicle registrations)

Exports

64

1955 59   63   67   71   75   79   83

Source: Nissan Motors, *Jidōsha sangyō handobukku* (Automobile Industry Handbook), 1985.

here the data show that its growth was primarily driven and sustained by domestic demand until at least 1969, when rapid growth was winding down.

Accordingly, it is my contention that Japan's rapid-growth economy was primarily powered by domestic demand. This is in no way to say or even imply that exports were unimportant. They were important, and the reason they were so important is to be found in natural resources.

Sadly lacking in natural resources domestically, Japan has had to rely upon imports to meet practically all of its natural resource needs. The immediate postwar experience illustrates how very devastating not being able to access these overseas resources can be for the economy. In 1946, Japan's GNP was a mere half of what it had been during the war. As that year's economic white paper astutely pointed out, this was not so much because the war had wiped out the bulk of Japan's manufacturing capacity as it was because the country was unable to import raw materials. This postwar experience highlighted again how very vital resource imports are for the Japanese economy.

If you want to import resources, you have to pay for them somehow, and that means you need at least equivalent exports. Importing more than you export soon brings you up against the balance of payments ceiling, which then means you have to rein in your imports, which curtails your growth. By the same token, the only way the ceiling can be raised is by expanding exports. In that sense—in that they enabled Japan to import raw material resources—exports were an important factor in sustaining Japan's rapid growth. While they may not have been the star of the show, they were, along with the high savings rate, certainly an important supporting actor.

So much, then, for the mechanisms that enabled this rapid growth. The structural basis understood, it is important to look next at one of the economic problems that this rapid growth engendered: inflation.

Wholesale and Consumer Price Inflation

As explained above, Japan's rapid growth was led and powered by industrial growth. Vigorous capital investment plus technological innovation enabled industry to achieve spectacular productivity advances. In the process, labor flowed from agriculture, which was unable to achieve equivalent productivity gains, to industry. This inevitably created a disparity between wholesale prices and retail prices.

There is a very wide variety of goods and services, each with its own price. The cost of an apple, taxi fare, and more are all prices. Moreover, all of these prices vary from region to region, giving us even more prices to consider. When all of these very different prices are compiled and a weighted average calculated, that average is the price index. There are two main price indices: the wholesale price index (now called the corporate goods price index) and the consumer price index. Among the items in the wholesale price index are resource inputs such as steel, machinery, petroleum, and chemical products and a wide range of manufactured products. The consumer price index obviously includes the prices of the things that retail consumers purchase for their own use. About half of the consumer price index items are foodstuffs (agricultural products in the broad sense), and the rest are other goods and services such as train and taxi fares and the price of a haircut.

Oddly, these two indices did not move in tandem during the rapid-growth years. Wholesale prices rose only 4 percent for the entire 13 years from 1951 to 1964. Indeed, it would not be far wrong to say that the wholesale price index was basically flat in that period. By contrast, the consumer price index rose on average by more than 4 percent *per year*—a total increase of 60

Table 19. Wholesale prices vs. consumer prices

(1951 base)

	Wholesale price index	Consumer price index
1951	100.0	100.0
1952	101.9	104.7
1953	102.6	112.1
1954	101.9	118.7
1955	100.1	118.8
1956	104.5	119.7
1957	107.6	123.1
1958	100.6	123.8
1959	101.6	125.4
1960	102.8	129.9
1961	103.8	135.7
1962	102.1	144.7
1963	103.9	155.2
1964	104.1	161.7

Sources: Bank of Japan Statistics Bureau for wholesale price index (weighted average), Management and Coordination Agency for consumer price index (urban and rural combined).

percent—during this period. Why was there such a disparity between the wholesale price index and the consumer price index?

In his 1966 *Nihon keizai wa dō naru ka* (Where Is the Japanese Economy Going? [Iwanami Shinsho]), the economist Ōuchi Hyōe offered the view that such a gap was bound to be temporary:

I remember Ikeda Hayato's dismissing the criticism and complaints about the rise in consumer prices by pointing out that wholesale prices were not going up all that much and saying consumer prices would come down as productivity improved and more goods became available. This was dismissed as "Ikeda economics" and derided as "bourgeois." Admittedly, there was a period when consumer prices rose and wholesale prices fell, but it was myopic to build on this to claim that there was no inflation over the past decade or even just the last few years. There was, but I think Minobe Ryōkichi pretty much nailed it when he said that wholesale prices and consumer prices may diverge for a while but there is no way the two can be wildly disconnected within a single economy. Almost by definition, wholesale prices and consumer prices have to be linked and have to move more or less in tandem over the long run.

Besides Ōuchi, there were those who argued that, since wholesale prices are the prices companies pay and consumer prices are the prices consumers pay, the divergence of consumer prices rising faster than wholesale prices demonstrates that consumers were exploited. Yet all of these premises are flawed.

The divergence between the wholesale price index and the consumer price index simply means that the agricultural and service sectors were slower to achieve enhanced productivity than the manufacturing sector that led the economic growth.

One has only to compare the productivity gains in the iron and steel industry with the productivity gains made by barbers to understand this. Even though productivity levels differ, the incomes earned by workers in the two industries are essentially the same. (If there were major income disparities, all the barbers would be working in the steel industry or all the steelworkers would be cutting hair.) Prices have to be higher in the agricultural and service sectors than in manufacturing to provide equivalent income levels.

This is why there was inflation in consumer prices even though wholesale prices held relatively steady. The same phenomenon may be observed in almost every country, the disparity was just particularly noticeable in Japan. In the United States, for example, the wholesale price index (called the producer price index in the US) was 110 and the consumer price index was 119 in 1964 (both calculated from a base of 100 in 1951). This is a much smaller disparity than that of the Japanese price indices shown in Table 19, and the Japanese figures are actually much closer to the equivalent figures for Italy, which were 118 and 165.

The point, however, is that the disparity between the two indices in no way means that companies are profiting unreasonably or that consumers are being cheated somehow. Rather, it shows that manufacturing companies invested heavily in new plant and equipment and achieved considerable productivity enhancements. Once this is understood, it should be easy to see why the sharp sector productivity differentials pushed the two indices apart and led to consumer price inflation in countries like Japan and Italy where rapid industrialization brought rapid growth.

To conclude this chapter, it is worth touching briefly on land prices.

After ballooning in the late 1980s, land prices in Japan went on to collapse in the 1990s. This experience has left the Japanese very wary of any sharp increase in land prices, with some people going on to think that any price surge is a speculative bubble waiting to burst. While there is much to laud about this wariness, it is not true that all land price increases are bubbles. Looking back at land prices in postwar Japan, the sharpest increase in the rapid-growth years was during the Iwato Boom (June 1958 to December 1961). This increase was due to sharply higher demand for and development of residential and other land in response to the rapid industrialization and the accompanying population flow into the major urban areas. The rise in land prices was a reflection of the Japanese economy's rapid growth, as was the rise in equity prices.

CHAPTER 6

Reactions Right and Left

Demonstration against the Japan-US Security Treaty, 1960. (© Kyodo News)

When the ballots from the first round of voting were tallied, it was Ikeda Hayato 246, Ishii Mitsujirō 196, and Fujiyama Aiichirō 49. In the second round, it was Ikeda 302 and Ishii 194. Thus it was that Ikeda was elected president of the Liberal Democratic Party on July 14, 1960, (and subsequently prime minister of Japan, given the LDP's majority in the Diet) and moved to form a new cabinet that might heal the bitter jockeying among the party's internal factions. Ikeda proved a strong leader right up until cancer forced his resignation in the October after the Tokyo Olympics ended, and his income-doubling plan was a good prescription for the economy. Indeed, he epitomized the idea of a man rising to the occasion. Very seldom in history has a leader emerged with such a clear platform so suited to the times. Ikeda came to the fore advocating that the Japanese put their political differences aside and concentrate on achieving economic prosperity. He was the right man for the season—a politician who, more than anyone else, symbolizes the era of rapid growth.

The 1950s: Politics to the Fore

In his 1985 *Gendai seiji: 1955 igo* (Contemporary Politics since 1955), political scientist Masumi Junnosuke wrote, "The Socialist movement was the most important political current in Japan in the 1950s."

With the special procurements related to the Korean War kickstarting growth, the economy embarked on its long rapid-growth march in the mid-1950s. Yet if the 1960s were the age of the economy, the 1950s were the age of politics. It was, after all, the defining feature of the 1950s that the Japan Socialist Party and other leftist forces constituted a very credible opposition to the dominant conservative policies. Although the Soviet Union's brutal subjugation of its East European satellites was on vivid display in Hungary in 1956, there was still a vast following looking to socialism for support, and Masumi's characterization remains valid. On the conservative side, the core longing seemed to be for Japanese rearmament once the San Francisco Peace Treaty took effect and Japan regained its independence. These were not, of course, the only points of left-right contention.

Although the socialist forces were thrown into disarray following the creation of the short-lived Katayama Tetsu coalition cabinet (May 1947 to March 1948), they regrouped in October 1955 with the right and left wings coming together to form the Japan Socialist Party. This gave the party 155, or nearly one-third, of the 467 seats in the House of Representatives and made them a force to be reckoned with. Influenced by business interests alarmed at the prospect of a united and growing left, the two conservative parties— Yoshida Shigeru's Liberal Party and Hatoyama Ichirō's Japan Democratic Party—merged in November 1955 to form the Liberal Democratic Party. Thus was born the 1955 system—with the LDP holding the reins of power and the JSP acting as the perennial opposition—which constituted the basic framework for Japanese politics for more than three decades.

The policy stance that the new LDP took was not the former Liberals' priority emphasis on economic development but rather the conservatives' emphasis on revising the Constitution with an eye toward rearmament. This showed up most clearly in the Kishi Nobusuke cabinet that came to power in 1957 and its push to revise the Japan-US Treaty of Mutual Cooperation and Security as a first step to rearmament. In preparation, an amendment to the Police Duties Execution Act was submitted to the Diet with no advance notice in October 1958. This amendment was aimed at sharply expanding and strengthening the powers of the police. In his memoirs, Kishi explained the amendment's purpose:

Expecting considerable opposition to revising the Security Treaty and determined to do everything I possibly could to put the opposition down, I thought amending the Police Act was an absolute prerequisite to maintaining order to that end. (*Kishi Nobusuke no kaisō* [Bungeishunjū, 1981])

The furor over the Security Treaty was already building, and on October 25 the *Tokyo Shimbun* ran an interview with Kishi in which he enumerated the three goals of (1) protecting the people's lives, health, and property, (2) deterring crime, and (3) maintaining public order. Kishi then clearly declared, "The main thing wanting at present is the authority to maintain public safety and order."

Kishi was determined to push this amendment, which many considered a return to the draconian prewar Peace Preservation Law, through the Diet, but Sōhyō (General Council of Trade Unions of Japan) called a general strike that brought out four million workers, the JSP put up a stalwart resistance, and the bill was given a quiet burial.

Having played a major part in the brutal administration of Manchukuo (the Japanese puppet state established in Manchuria in 1932) and later having served as minister of commerce and industry in the wartime cabinet of Tōjō Hideki, Kishi had been slated to be tried as a Class A war criminal but was instead released and turned to politics, winning a House of Representatives seat in 1953. As seen in his comments on the Police Act, he was thoroughly steeped in prewar thinking from head to toe. For him, the only way to rebuild postwar Japan was to recreate it based on the prewar model. Yet given that it was impossible to rewrite the Constitution along prewar lines so long as the JSP held a third of the Diet seats, Kishi set his sights on preparing for remilitarization while seeking to revise the Security Treaty with the United States.

Kishi faced opposition even within the conservative camp. Yoshida Shigeru publicly declared that he saw no need to revise the treaty. And unlike Kishi, Yoshida was strongly against the idea of military rearmament. Kishi was not entirely out of line in what he sought, in that the LDP platform included calls for "independent amendment of the Constitution" and "a self-defense force appropriate given the circumstances," but, as seen in Yoshida's comments, opinion was clearly divided even within the LDP on the extent to which Japan should rearm and the steps it should take toward that end. Kishi was a hard-liner on the far right even within his own party.

The 1960 Security Treaty Struggle and the Miike Struggle

The revised Japan-US Security Treaty was signed in Washington in January 1960 and submitted to the Diet for ratification the next month. However, it met fierce opposition and was only approved by the LDP members of the House of Representatives on May 20, with the opposition parties boycotting the session in protest. The LDP's steamrolling tactics further inflamed the already widespread opposition to Anpo (the abbreviated Japanese name of the treaty) and a general strike called for June 4 drew 4.6 million partici-pants—the largest strike since the end of the war. On June 11, there were 230,000 people demonstrating in front of the Diet, and the nationwide total of protesters reached 5.6 million on June 15. That evening, a group of rightists attacked a large group of primarily female demonstrators. Enraged at this, a group of student activists crashed the gate and entered the Diet grounds. Kanba Michiko, a female demonstrator, died in the melee. The House of Councilors not having explicitly rejected it, the revised Security Treaty went into effect one month later on June 19. This brought 6.2 million people out in protest on June 22, and Kishi resigned as prime minister the following day.

The Security Treaty issue spawned the largest and strongest national pro-test movement in Japan's postwar political history. Large numbers of Japanese were very wary of Japan's getting too involved in America's anticommunist strategies, and even more people were aghast at Kishi's high-handed, strong-arm political stance. As Masumi Junnosuke said, the Anpo struggle was "the most important Japanese political campaign of the 1950s" and "marked the high point for the Socialist movement."

While the Socialist movement had a clear purpose and justifiable cause in seeking to defend the "peace Constitution" and "postwar democracy," in backing the campaign to ban nuclear weapons, and in other political causes, it was very quickly found to harbor fundamental contradictions when it came to economic issues. All too often, the insistence that economic issues could only be ultimately and essentially resolved by achieving a socialist state ran up against everyday rationality, and economic struggles all too often morphed into take-no-prisoners political conflicts. This showed up in the movement's response to technical innovation and rationalization, for example.

As noted earlier, it was technological innovation and the willingness to invest in productivity enhancements (rationalization) that so enriched our lives. Yet the 1950s labor movement was focused on class warfare and ada-mantly opposed to innovation and rationalization. Typical of labor unions nationwide, the Yawata Steel union campaigned in 1956 under the banner of opposing productivity improvements at labor's expense. Although they would have done better to push for a fair share of a bigger economic pie, they spent their time and energy fighting the technological innovation and productivity enhancements that make the economic pie bigger. The idea of pushing for a larger share of a bigger pie is something that anyone should be able to under-stand and would have been a natural position for any company-wide union.

Yet anyone who suggested this approach was quickly shouted down and labeled "insufficiently committed to the class struggle" by people who prided themselves on their class consciousness. Going into the 1960s, however, the Yawata union changed its policy to "getting a fair share of the productivity gains." Then, in 1964, the Japan Council of Metalworkers' Unions was formed with an emphasis on labor-management cooperation.

There was one group within the Japan Socialist Party that was quick to take note of this change: the "structural reform" camp, whose members counted the Italian Communist Party leader Palmiro Togliatti among their influences. This camp, which included JSP Secretary General Eda Saburō, emerged very quickly in the wake of the 1960 Anpo struggle. Yet Sōhyō and the party's left wing denounced Eda and his followers for their reformist thinking and he was unable to exercise effective leadership within the party. As a result, the JSP proved unable to shed its 1950s style.

The 1959–60 strike at the Miike Mine in Kyushu proved catastrophic for this rigid ideological stance. The problems at Miike may have been further inflamed by the strong personality of the mining company's president with his engineering background and the targeting of union leaders for early retirement, but in retrospect it must be acknowledged that the core cause was the uncompromising political battle waged by a labor movement steeped in class-warfare ideology. In the big picture, it was impossible to halt the energy shift from coal to oil, and this shift made it inevitable that the coal industry would shrink, causing concurrent shrinkage in the number of miners needed. Thus the crucial issue here was how to seamlessly shift redundant coal miners to productive employment elsewhere. The labor unions' priorities should have been wresting the most advantageous terms for the redundant workers and ensuring that government policy was most protective of the people who were caught in the transition. Yet this was not how the theoreticians who guided the Miike union (notably Kyushu University professor and leftist ideologue Sakisaka Itsurō), the Sōhyō leadership, and others in the labor movement saw the issue.

Moderate-left economist Arisawa Hiromi, who visited Miike in the midst of the turmoil, recounted:

> I explained that this is essentially an energy shift issue and that people who cling unthinkingly to coal are going to be run over by oil. I explained that this reality has to be acknowledged in formulating

struggle objectives and the focus should be on how to ensure a smooth transition for our people. . . . I emphasized that the energy revolution means that coal is increasingly going to be supplanted by oil and that this means a struggle wedded to coal is a no-win position. I said this is basic economics and, while I did not talk about withdrawing from the field, I did talk about the need to find satisfactory closure. And I said I would do whatever I could to help but that I could not go along with the insistence that coal had to be preserved come what may. (*Sengo keizai o kataru: Shōwa-shi e no shōgen* [University of Tokyo Press, 1989])

Yet Arisawa's views found no traction at all with the Miike union, fervent in its adherence to the Sakisaka line, or with the Sōhyō leadership. They saw the Miike struggle as part of an epic showdown between Japan's capitalists and its workers, and they aimed to turn Miike into a base for the revolution. This was a suicide mission.

On July 19, 1960, the Ikeda cabinet that had taken the reins after Kishi resigned moved quickly to deal with the Miike issue, and the Central Labor Relations Commission narrowly averted a clash between the picketers and the police at 3:00 a.m. the very next day. The Miike struggle, which had lasted for over 280 days, was brought to a close on November 1, bringing down the curtain on the Anpo-Miike age of politics with the union having gained nothing for all its troubles.

The Income-Doubling Plan

In sharp contrast to the Kishi cabinet and its highly politicized emphasis on revising the Constitution and paving the way for rearmament, Ikeda took a lower profile and made the economy his priority. "Leave the economics to me," he said. The income-doubling plan was the centerpiece of his program.

Pessimism about Japan's economic future prevailed in the late 1950s, with most observers arguing that the growth rate would fall off sooner or later once the postwar reconstruction demand ebbed. Many also contended that Japan would soon run up against its balance of payments ceiling if imports continued to increase commensurate with economic growth and that the economy did not have sufficient export competitiveness to raise the balance of payments ceiling and sustain strong growth. Such was the thinking among Japanese economists. It was in keeping with this crisis mentality that the

Ikeda Hayato
(© Kyodo News)

Shimomura Osamu
(© Kyodo News)

author of the 1956 Economic White Paper coined the famous "Our postwar is over" phrase to emphasize that the recovery and reconstruction phase was over and that Japan would need tremendous innovation if it wanted to keep the growth rate from collapsing. Within the general gloom, Shimomura Osamu, an economist with the Ministry of Finance, stood out as extremely optimistic about the economy's future and is generally is credited as the chief architect of Ikeda's income-doubling plan.

Writing in *Keizai seichō jitsugen no tame ni* (How to Achieve Economic Growth), a report dated September 17, 1958, for internal distribution within the ministry, Shimomura argued:

> The Japanese economy is at an important turning point. For some years following the war, we have been concerned almost to the point of obsession with how to hold aggregate demand within the aggregate supply parameters. Yet the issue now before us is rather that of how to manage our sufficient supply capacity wisely for sound economic growth.

Shimomura later recalled the circumstances that led him to perceive this "turning point" for the economy as a springboard for growth:

> Many economists extrapolate from trend lines going back to the Meiji era (1868–1912). But if you do that, you end up seeing everything and explaining everything based upon those trend lines. Likewise, you end up projecting future circumstances from past or present circumstances.

In order to allow for the possibility that events will unfold differently, we must determine what lies ahead by looking at today's conditions, the conditions that are currently being created, and the new conditions that have shown up. I would suggest that the situation today is a stage in the process of moving rapidly to a higher dimension. In economic terms, the present is a staging ground for advancing apace from our current sorry state to being an advanced industrial country—a situation totally unlike anything we have experienced to date. I think that "springboard for growth" expresses this situation perfectly. (*Shōgen: Kōdo seichōki no Nihon*, vol. 1, compiled by *Shūkan Ekonomisuto* [Economist Weekly], 1984)

Early the following year (1959), the *Yomiuri Shimbun* published theoretical economist Nakayama Ichirō's "Chingin nibai o teishō" (Call for Wage Doubling) in its January 3 edition. Nakayama wrote:

How best to approach the ideal of a welfare state in the midst of poverty? In thinking about this, it is imperative we first seek to be as specific as possible about what we want the future to look like. In seeking to envision some specifics, I am calling for an economy in which wages are double what they are today. . . . Obviously, there are prerequisites to doubling wages, the first of which is achieving productivity worth twice as much. While Japanese wages are currently about one-third West German levels, West Germany is able to afford this threefold discrepancy because it has three times the productivity we do. Wage levels that do not reflect and are not in line with productivity levels are untenable, no matter how much we might dictate them. . . . Japan has been impoverished for a long time now. Yet the difference between the past and the present lies in whether or not we are aware of this poverty. In the present situation, now that people are aware of this, we cannot simply push forward on the assumption the situation will not change. Communism seeks to resolve this situation with violence. If we are to avoid that path, it is essential we formulate alternative solutions. I believe the doubling of wages—by serving first as a goal shared by labor and management alike and eventually becoming a policy objective for the government—can be an effective step toward the achievement of a concrete vision for Japan's future.

Nakayama Ichirō's call for doubling wages in the January 3, 1959, *Yomiuri Shimbun.*

Serving as Minister of International Trade and Industry in the Kishi cabinet, Ikeda quickly unveiled his own proposal for doubling wages. At the time, Shimomura was already providing ideas and insights for Ikeda. Not long afterward, in November, Prime Minister Kishi called upon his economic advisory council to come up with a long-term program for doubling national income. With the prime minister preoccupied with the Anpo issue, it fell to Ikeda to take the lead in planning for growth. When the economist Tsuru Shigeto took to the pages of the weekly *Asahi Jānaru* (*Asahi Journal*) to criticize the proposal to double monthly salaries, Ikeda rushed fearlessly to its defense in an article titled "Bokkōki ni aru Nihon keizai" (The Japanese Economy on the Growth Springboard), published in the August 2, 1959, issue of the same magazine:

Professor Tsuru acknowledges that the Japanese economy achieved strong growth in the postwar recovery and reconstruction period. How did we do that?

First was the strong consensus on the need for recovery and reconstruction. Second was that large numbers of workers with advanced technical skills were given the opportunity to return to work. Third was the rapid recovery of production equipment stock. And fourth was the strong pressure from pent-up demand.

These factors are not exclusive to the recovery and reconstruction period. More generally, they are characteristic of an economic take-off period and the Japanese economy today is very clearly exhibiting all the features of an economic take-off period. . . . Professor Tsuru has apparently asked if I am so confident of this that I will unhesitatingly resign my government position if we are unable to double monthly salaries over the course of the next decade and has apparently asserted that there are some bureaucrats in some socialist countries who have had to resign when they were unable to meet their productivity targets. I must say that this is very unlike Professor Tsuru and betrays an outmoded and rather mistaken concept of taking responsibility. While it seems only natural that economic planning officials in a socialist country would resign if they were unable to fulfill their plans, is it really fair to equate economic policy officials in free-market economies with their counterparts in socialist control economies? I have no intention of shirking or evading responsibility for what I do, but given that I am not advocating a command economy or a control economy, I am not saying or even thinking we should mandate doubling monthly salaries within 10 years. However, I will say I will not only resign my government post but will resign from politics, which has been my whole life until now, if my policies are followed and salaries do not double within 10 years.

One of the fundamental problems that many economists, and especially those on the left, saw as bedeviling the Japanese economy was the "dual structure" wage disparity between the giant companies and the smaller companies. This was another issue Tsuru raised. In his August 2 article, Ikeda responded:

While income disparity is a serious problem, I do not think the proper response is to be found in either "lament not the poverty but the inequality" thinking akin to that of the wartime state-of-emergency economy or stagnant feudal economic thinking. The effort to shrink the inequality should be made within the context of growing the economy and expanding aggregate production. Generally speaking, we should try to understand the issues of economic growth—including the question of what to do about the "dual structure"—and look for solutions within the context of the dynamic growth process itself.

There is no question but that Shimomura was working with Ikeda behind the scenes and that Ikeda based much of his discourse on Shimomura's thinking. Ikeda concluded his article by saying that he would leave it to Shimomura to write about the quantitative analysis of the factors of production elsewhere. This "elsewhere" was a separate article by Shimomura in the *Asahi Journal*. The fact that Shimomura wrote a separate article makes it hard to credit the idea that Ikeda's article was ghostwritten by Shimomura. Ikeda was a recognized economist fully capable of doing battle with the doubting economists on his own.

After succeeding Kishi as prime minister in July 1960, Ikeda promptly set to work refining his income-doubling plan. In an interview printed in *Shōgen: Kōdo seichōki no Nihon*, Shimomura recalled the process of putting this plan together:

> Now, of course, you could use computers for much of this, but when we were drawing the plan up, we had a giant table with all the data. This showed us all the numbers for if GNP doubled or tripled over the course of the decade. The numbers were all there for the expected changes in consumption, fiscal spending, and everything else. It was a very comprehensive table. And because there was so much there, it was essential that the calculations be done consistently, which was really a lot of work, but we had people who could do it. Ikeda would come in, watch a while, make a comment or two, and then leave.
>
> *It's been said that this table was big enough to fill a 10 m² room. Is that true?*
> **Shimomura**: No, it wasn't like that. It was a set of tables printed on separate pages. And I doubt it would have been a whole 10 m² even if we laid them all out together.

The cabinet formally ratified the income-doubling plan on December 27,

1960, at the Economic Council's recommendation. The plan posited an average annual 7.2 percent growth rate over the next 10 years, which would yield a doubling over the course of the decade. Many economists, including many within the government itself, thought the plan was overly optimistic, but Ikeda was not satisfied with this "moderate" growth and pledged to work for 9 percent growth. This was separate from the plan as ratified by the cabinet. Shimomura thought an even higher number—11 percent—was a reasonable growth target. In fact, the Japanese economy achieved an average of 10.5 percent annual growth over the course of the next 10 years, very close to Shimomura's figure.

Japan's rapid growth was not a product of the income-doubling plan. Indeed, it is safe to say that that it could not have been, inasmuch as Japan does not have a command economy. Still, it is very significant that politicians and bureaucrats responsible for policy management were able to see the 10 percent growth potential in the architecture of economic growth as outlined in the previous chapter. On the other side, left-wing opinion leaders continued to expound Marxist dogma throughout the 1960s.

Rapid Economic Growth and Political Party Approval
The year after the Olympics, 1965, saw Japan experience the worst downturn of the whole rapid-growth period. This was the same year crisis-ridden Yamaichi Securities, one of the leading brokerages, became the first company in history to receive special bridge financing from the Bank of Japan. Even so, this was just a slump and not a contraction, the figure for real GNP growth being 6.4 percent, which is very respectable by today's standards. Two Marxist economists providing theoretical underpinning for the left wing of the JSP discussed the situation:

Ōuchi Hyōei: I really think the government should just ignore this downturn. Let the capitalists make the effort and deal with it as capitalists. It would be good for them to bleed a bit. But Japanese capitalist politics—which is to say LDP politics—is not going to let this run its course. In reality, none of Japan's capitalists is capable of the sort of initiative I'm thinking of. They are all going to run crying to the government for succor. And the government is going to help them out. This is what passes for government demand creation and fiscal policy.

Minobe Ryōkichi: You think Japanese capitalism would survive even without government intervention?

Ōuchi: Not only would it survive, it would recover sooner if the government would leave it alone.

Minobe: As capitalism?

Ōuchi: As capitalism. As healthier capitalism. Of course, there could be an immediate crisis and some companies could go down if the government kept its hands off, but if some companies collapse because of the downturn, so be it. If we have excess production capacity, the crisis might cause some companies to shed some of their excess. This might be painful for the companies in question, but it would be better in the long run if it meant getting rid of the old, low-productivity facilities. I really don't see any other way out of this situation. And if this triggers a recession, better now than later, because today's recession will be shallower and less painful than the inevitable recession later. If you're sick, the answer is not just to treat the symptoms or call for transfusions. Let nature take its course.

Minobe: But a recession now would be disastrous.

Ōuchi: It certainly would not be pretty. But that's reaping what you sow. Some people are going to have to learn some hard lessons.

It may be because it was in conversation, but Ōuchi was very clear about his thinking here. From the Marxist standpoint, there is no hope for capitalism; we just have to wait for the advent of a socialist society. Nor is there any game plan for a productive economic struggle by labor, which is the ultimate irony, coming as it does from a movement that is supposed to represent labor's interests.

Rapid economic growth did not necessarily create conditions favorable to the LDP. Voter support for conservative candidates fell steadily from 50 percent in the early 1950s to 35 percent in 1970. Ishikawa Masumi attributed this straight-line decline in conservative voter support during the rapid-growth years to labor mobility. His intriguing thesis deserves to be quoted here.

> Why did voter support for the LDP and conservative candidates decline with labor mobility? And why did voter support hold steady once this labor mobility ended? In simplified schematic terms, I suspect this can be explained as follows.
> The basis of support for the conservative parties is to be found not

in the party organization but in the organizations that support the individual candidates, which are typically set up at the local level. So it is local community leaders who bring in the votes with messages like "Candidate X has done a lot for our village" or "Let's rely on candidate Y." In rural areas, these organizations might be seen as occupation-based leagues of farmers aiming to protect their occupational interests, but they are essentially local community interest groups. Consequently, even if someone quits farming and goes to work in a local factory, he is still going to support "our" candidate.

It is only when voters move out of the village and take up residence in a different electoral district that they lose their peer-group allegiance to the local candidate—and they are very seldom recruited to join the support group for the conservative candidate running in the new, urban district. This is a weakness in the party organization. Having no village identification in the urban area they move to, these people often no longer bother voting. (*Dēta sengo seiji-shi* [Iwanami Shinsho, 1984])

Going into the 1970s, the destinations for labor mobility moved from manufacturing to construction, services, and other nonmanufacturing industries. As a result, there were more nonfarm employment opportunities closer to home and the population exodus stopped, and with it the drop-off in LDP voter support. This is how Ishikawa explains it.

Even so, why was it that the urban "proletariat" did not move to support the JSP? Essentially, as I noted above, it was because Marxist ideology, while perhaps able to draw up a game plan for a political struggle, is unable to envision an economic struggle that would be in the workers' interests and would lead to an improved standard of living.

There was no essentially transformative crisis at any point during the rapid-growth era—nor has there been one in the years since then, for that matter. Not only did average incomes rise 10 percent year after year, there was greater income equalization throughout the period. (In this respect, Japan's rapid growth differed from China's current rapid growth.)

This change also showed up in surveys of how people perceived their social status. There has always been a substantial level of middle-class identification in Japan, but in 1965, the share of the broad middle class (including those who rated their status as upper-middle, middle, and lower-middle) had risen to 86 percent of the population. Even farming villages, which were considered

Table 20. Self-identification by social stratum (%)

	Upper	Upper-middle	Middle	Lower-middle	Lower	Don't know, no answer
1958	0	4	37	32	17	10
1965	1	7	50	29	8	5

Source: Public Opinion Survey on the Life of the People, Cabinet Secretariat, as cited in the Economic Planning Agency's 1973 White Paper on the National Lifestyle.

synonymous with poverty before and during the war, suddenly became communities of working landowners and joined to form the conservative base. Given this social upheaval, the old 1950s-style political struggle between capitalism and socialism—between capital and labor—was rendered essentially meaningless. Yet having expelled the reformists from their party, the Socialists held to their old ways and sunk slowly into irrelevance. In contrast, the Liberal Democrats were able to set aside their internal differences and establish the groundwork for stable, long-term rule against the backdrop of rapid economic growth. Were it not for the benefits accruing from this growth, the LDP would have seen major declines in both voter support and Diet seats.

Into the 1970s

The distortions introduced by rapid growth—notably urban overcrowding and pollution—gradually became evident for all to see in the latter half of the 1960s, and people began to reject these side effects and the growth mindset that apparently spawned them. This rejection took many forms, among them citizen protests and the election of progressive governors. Left-leaning economist and Tokyo University of Education Professor Minobe Ryōkichi was elected governor of Tokyo with support from the JSP and the Japanese Communist Party on a platform of eliminating the distortions. Minobe, who took office on April 1, 1967, was the first of Japan's progressive governors, but he was soon followed by others in Osaka, Okinawa, Saitama, Kanagawa, and elsewhere. By 1975, there were 10 such progressive governors nationwide.

Yet even as these progressives were being elected to lead at the prefectural level, the JSP continued its decline on the national stage, suffering a defeat of historic proportions in the December 1969 House of Representatives election, falling from 140 seats to 90 seats after the votes were counted. By contrast, the LDP ended up with a massive 300 seats. While voters, especially in the heavily urban areas, were sharply critical of the threats to their own lives, the infrastructure inadequacies, and the unbridled development, they voted at the national level for the framework of stability that the conservatives provided.

Having continued for well over a decade, Japan's rapid growth was drawing to a close in 1970 when the international "Progress and Harmony for Mankind" exposition was held in Osaka. While the causes of this economic slowing have been detailed in the previous chapter, it should be noted that this was also a time of dramatic upheaval in the international environment impacting Japan. In 1971, US Secretary of State Henry Kissinger paid a secret visit to China, paving the way for President Richard Nixon to visit the next year. America and China had been the bitterest of enemies ever since the Korean War—so much so that it was illegal at one point for Americans to collect Chinese stamps—yet here their leaders were suddenly shaking hands. That same year, in what became known as "the Nixon shock," Nixon suspended the dollar's convertibility into gold in August, which led to the collapse of the postwar Bretton Woods system of fixed exchange rates. The yen was revalued from its long-standing rate of 360 to the dollar to 308 to the dollar and Japan and other major countries subsequently shifted to the current system of floating exchange rates.

In July 1972, Satō Eisaku stepped down after a record-setting seven years and eight months as prime minister. He was succeeded by Tanaka Kakuei. While Tanaka fully justified his reputation as a "computerized bulldozer" in normalizing relations with China that same year, his domestic policies were largely those that he had set forth in his book *Nihon rettō kaizō-ron* (1972; English translation *Building a New Japan* published by Simul Press in 1973). It is instructive to quote from his preface.

[T]he rapid economic growth that began in the last half of the 1950's brought about an excessive concentration of population and industry along the Pacific coast, transforming Japan into a unique society of high population density. While the big cities suffer from the pains and irritations of overcrowding, rural areas suffer from the exodus of youth and the resultant loss of vital energy for growth. Rapid urbanization has bred increasing numbers of people who have never known the joys of rural life, chasing rabbits in the mountains, fishing for crucian carp in streams, whose only home is a tiny apartment in some huge city. With such a situation, how can we pass on to future generations the qualities and traditions of the Japanese people?

At this centennial point of the Meiji Restoration, the advantages of urban concentration are clearly being overwhelmed by the disadvantages. Public opinion calls for the simultaneous solution of overcrowding and underpopulation to live in comfort in a beautiful land of affluence and security. To achieve these ends, we must boldly reverse this torrential urban concentration and direct our national energy and surplus economic strength to remodeling the entire archipelago. Disparity between urban and rural areas, between the prosperous Pacific coast and the stagnating Japan Sea coast, can surely be eliminated by using levers such as relocating industries, making them more knowledge-intensive, constructing super-express railways and trunk expressways throughout the nation, and creating nationwide information and communications networks. (*Building a New Japan*, pp. iii–iv)

Building upon this vision, Tanaka went on to write in the body of the book:

Many people now believe that the period of rapid growth for the Japanese economy is over. However, even though we may not be able to expect any large increase in either private plant and equipment investment or exports, there are still a number of factors sufficient to support continued economic growth.

The first is the expansion of infrastructure investment. . . .

If we work to shift the traditional course of economic growth from one based on private investment and exports to one with the priority on welfare and increased social overhead expenditures, the economy still has great growth potential. (Ibid., pp. 60–61)

It was, however, impossible to create economic growth with construction projects alone, and the rapid-growth era was already over. Tanaka's ambitious plans to remodel the archipelago simply created a construction boom and a spike in land prices. In 1973, the rise in consumer prices topped 11 percent and people saw this as rampant inflation. Whereas Ikeda's income-doubling plan had defined an era, Tanaka's remodeling plan turned out to be just another campaign platform.

Children heading to school in Yokkaichi, masked because of the noxious fumes from the smokestacks. (© Kyodo News)

Rapid economic growth completely changed our lives, leaving a legacy both good and bad in its wake. This chapter looks at both the positives and the negatives, focusing on the longer life expectancies it enabled and the pollution it exacerbated.

Longer Lifespans

The average Japanese life expectancy in 2009 was 80 years for males and 86 years for females. For the population as a whole, it was 83, the longest in the world. Although you would expect living longer to be a primary concern of all people everywhere, there are still major disparities around the globe despite the global access to information and the striking advances being made in medical care. In China, for example, a next-door neighbor, the average life expectancy is still only 74; in India, it is 65; and in Russia, the average male life expectancy is a mere 62. In Chad, life expectancy is low but with almost no gender imbalance: 47 for males, 48 for females.

A nation's average life expectancy is determined by more than the advances in and spread of medical science, as there is a wide range of economic and social factors that also come into play. Among them, economic growth (as reflected in higher incomes) is one of the most important. Looking quickly at average life expectancies around the globe, it is clear that the industrialized countries with higher per-capita incomes outperform the less developed and developing countries. It also appears that, by and large, economic development and average life expectancy moved in tandem after World War II. This is shown in Figure 13, which also shows how Japan was a leader in extending its average life expectancy figures.

Looking back at the early 1950s when Japan's economic growth was just

Figure 13. Male and female life expectancy in selected countries

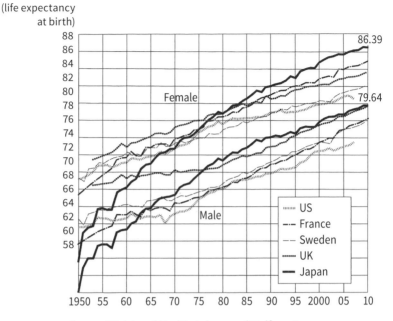

Source: Ministry of Health, Labour and Welfare, Japan.

getting started, we see that the average life expectancy was 59.6 for males and 63.0 for females. These figures seem very low in comparison with our friends, neighbors, and even ourselves today. By 1975, when the rapid-growth era had drawn to a close, life expectancy had risen to 71.7 for males and 76.9 for females. In little over two decades, the male life expectancy had grown 12 years and the female 14 years. In the two decades that followed (from 1975 to 1994), the male life expectancy added another five years and the female another six years, showing that life expectancy growth, like economic growth itself, had dulled.

What accounts for this rapid lengthening of Japanese life expectancy during the rapid-growth years? In attempting to answer this question, it is first necessary to look at longer-term trends. Even though we realize that medical advances and economic growth have progressed in uneven spurts, people tend to think that the growth in life expectancy has been linear over the course of history. A false assumption generally, it is particularly misleading in Japan's case. Abandoning easy assumptions, this section looks at

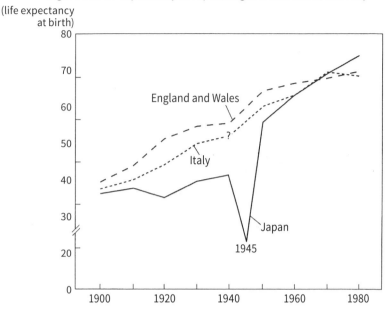

Figure 14. Life expectancy in Japan, England and Wales, and Italy

(life expectancy at birth)

England and Wales

Italy

Japan

1945

Source: Ministry of Health, Labour and Welfare, Japan.

Japanese male life expectancy over the years drawing upon the work done by University of California Professors S. Ryan Johansson and Carl Mosk.

Figure 14 charts the changes in life expectancy for Japan, Great Britain (England and Wales), and Italy from 1900 to 1980. In the early part of the century, Japan's per capita income was only one-eighth to one-fifth the figure for Great Britain. Despite this, the two countries' life expectancies were not that different, with Japan at 43 and Britain at 45. Its high per capita income notwithstanding, Britain lagged in hygiene and sanitation, and this was compounded by rampant urbanization; hence the low life expectancy. In contrast, Johansson and Mosk explain, Japan was able to offset its lower per capita income because the Meiji government had made a strong policy push in public hygiene and sanitation and because Japan was not as far along on the road to industrialization and urbanization. As a result, developing Japan boasted a life expectancy essentially on a par with that of the world's richest country around the beginning of the twentieth century.

And then, while the Italian and British life expectancies grew steadily longer for the next three decades, Japan basically stood still. Japanese average life expectancy for males in 1899–1903 was 44.0. In 1926–30, it was 44.8. Even though steady economic growth yielded higher per capita incomes, this was offset by the dual impact of industrialization and urbanization. Although the government did implement rudimentary public hygiene policies, it was hell-bent on militarization and unwilling to spend the sums needed for water and sewer systems, hospital modernization, and the like. At least in terms of life expectancy, Japan was a stagnant nation.

It is worth looking here at why urbanization has a negative impact on life expectancy. We tend to think of urban areas as pace-setters and rural areas as laggards, but Japanese urban areas had higher illness incidence rates and higher mortality rates than rural areas during the modernization process. Because cities had high population concentrations, urban life was much more dangerous than rural life.

As Johansson and Mosk note, we also need to look at rising income levels and the role of public hygiene. I suspect most readers would naturally be receptive to the idea that higher incomes and public hygiene both contribute to longer life expectancies, and I too think this hypothesis is straightforward and credible. Yet there are some scholars in the field, most particularly laissez-faire economists, who would beg to differ.

Led by the Chicago school, these neoclassical economists emphasize the importance of individual choice in the marketplace and generally disparage any government role. As such, they are loath to admit that public hygiene, a function of government policy, contributes to extending lifespans. University of Chicago economic historian Robert W. Fogel, who shared the Nobel Prize for Economics in 1993, is a leading proponent of this school. His position is that enhanced income contributes to enhanced life expectancy only in that it expands individual options, such as the options of eating better food and living in a better house. Yet it is undeniable that economic growth (enhanced income) also contributes by sustaining public (government) spending to prevent contagion, improve the water and sewer infrastructure, provide health insurance, and more; and Fogel's contention that enhanced income only contributes through the mechanism of personal choice is clearly flawed.

Disastrous in so many ways, World War II was also a disaster for Japan in terms of life expectancy. Near the end of the war, the government estimated that the average male life expectancy was 24 years. Yet in the early 1950s, a mere five or six years after the war ended, the male life expectancy was 59.6

and female life expectancy 63.0. Where it had taken 40 years to achieve a mere four-year increase in life expectancy before the war, life expectancies were increased a full 12 years in just the first half-dozen or so years after the war. This was primarily due to the discovery and availability of penicillin and other new medicines. Also significant was the dramatic decline in the number of young people contracting tuberculosis, as BCG vaccination became a standard procedure. Indeed, in one of modern medicine's striking success stories, tuberculosis was more or less eradicated by 1955.

It was when these medical successes were having their initial impact that economic growth got off the ground. Despite the dramatic improvement achieved during the first five or six years after the war, Japanese life expectancy was unable to recover fully from the stagnation war had imposed upon it and still lagged five years or more behind the industrialized West, as shown in Figure 13.

Infant Mortality and Health Insurance

Infant mortality was another important factor for life expectancy that showed major improvement starting in the 1950s in tandem with economic growth. As noted earlier, the crowded urban areas were long considered more dangerous in mortality terms than the rural areas because they had higher infection rates and higher mortality rates. Yet starting in the early 1950s, for the first time in Japanese history, and continuing from then on, the urban areas showed lower mortality rates than the rural areas did. While the population concentration meant the urban areas still had higher infection rates, the higher incomes meant they were able to offset this with more nutritious diets, better housing, and superior medical care. As a result, the migration from farm to city became a contributing factor to lower overall mortality rates.

The decline in the infant mortality rate is instrumental to understanding how economic factors played out to extend life expectancy in the rapid-growth years. As shown in Table 21, infant mortality dropped dramatically after the war. These health gains have been maintained, and Japan is widely recognized today as a world leader for its low infant mortality. This record is the product of two periods of accomplishment: the quarter century from 1950 to 1975, during which Japan achieved a truly dramatic reduction in its infant mortality rate, and the subsequent decade, during which the improvement in absolute numbers was not as striking but the percentage decline was no less

Table 21. Infant mortality per 1,000 births

1950	60.1	1986	5.2
1955	39.8	1987	5.0
1960	30.7	1988	4.8
1965	18.5	1989	4.6
1970	13.1	1990	4.6
1975	10.0	1991	4.4
1980	7.5	1992	4.5
1985	5.5	1993	4.3
		1994	4.2

Source: Public Opinion Survey on the Life of the People, Cabinet Secretariat, as cited in the Economic Planning Agency's 1973 White Paper on the National Lifestyle.

significant. During this latter period, the gains were largely attributable to advances in natal and prenatal care, as seen in the medical technologies for saving premature babies.

As medical care was improved, the efforts to reduce the infant mortality rate during the rapid-growth period were assisted in a number of ways by the higher income levels that this growth produced. Research by Ogura Seiritsu and Suzuki Reiko drawing upon extensive data at the prefectural, municipal, and county levels in the 1950–65 period has shown that (1) the increased percentage of deliveries at hospitals and other medical clinics was, along with the spread of water and sewer infrastructure, a factor in lowering the infant mortality rate and (2) the move to delivery in medical institutions was itself heavily influenced by the increase in real per capita income, as well as such factors as the mother's education level, the availability of hospital beds, and health insurance coverage. As noted in Chapter 1, some 97 percent of Japanese babies were delivered at home in 1950. Even in Tokyo, an outlier for having so many deliveries taking place in hospitals and other specialist institutions, this figure was 78 percent. In Kyoto, which had the second-highest percentage of institutional deliveries, the home-delivery figure was 91 percent. While there was some urban-rural disparity, home delivery was far and away the more common choice throughout Japan.

It was from this starting point that the percentage of deliveries carried out at medical facilities rose to its present high level, and the increasing reliance on medical facilities was largely influenced by the rise in per capita income. Recognizing that the other factors to which Ogura and Suzuki assign considerable weight—such as the mother's educational level and the availability of hospital beds—themselves vary depending upon the income level of the individual household and the community, it is clear that income's importance goes well beyond its direct impact.

This is borne out by the disparities in the different prefectures' infant mortality rates. In 1950, the infant mortality rates were 9.5 percent in Aomori, 9.0 percent in Iwate, and 8.0 percent in Akita—all very high percentages. In contrast, they were lower in the more urban prefectures: 4.4 percent in Tokyo and 4.1 percent in Kanagawa. This is a discrepancy of over 4.5 percentage points on average for the two groups, reflecting prefectural income disparities that were far greater before the rapid-growth period than they are today. Rapid growth sharply reduced these income and infant mortality disparities, bringing infant mortality down to 2.9 percent in Aomori and 1.4 percent in Tokyo and reducing the gap to 1.5 percentage points.

The prevalence of pneumonia was a significant factor in the high infant mortality rates in the Tōhoku region's Aomori, Iwate, and Akita prefectures. Thatched roofs have a certain charm and are looked back upon with a large dose of wistful nostalgia today, but the thatched roofs and loose-fitting shutters of traditional houses let in chill winds that often blew young lives away. With economic growth, housing materials and construction methods both improved to produce houses that, while perhaps not as aesthetically pleasing, were better insulated and more protective of young lives during the Tōhoku region's bitter winters.

One other major change that took place during the rapid-growth years was the establishment of a national health insurance system extending coverage to the entire population. Japan's social insurance system got its start with the 1922 Health Insurance Act designed to provide coverage for industrial workers, and it was gradually broadened and improved throughout the wartime and postwar years. However, public health insurance still did not cover farmers and other self-employed people—about a third of the population—as late as 1955 when Japan's rapid growth was getting started. This was a major impetus for the 1958 amendments that created the National Health Insurance Act and the 1961 move to "universal" health insurance extending coverage to all.

What impact did universal national health insurance have on life expectancy? In discussing this, I would like to reference research by Negishi Tatsuo and Naitō Masako. Figure 15 looks at morbidity, the treatment rate, and the

Figure 15. Morbidity, treatment, and mortality by age cohort, 1955

(per 100,000 people)

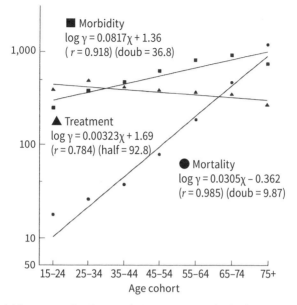

Source: Negishi Tatsuo and Naitō Masako "Genjō to sono haikei kara mita 21-seiki no iryō seido," in Uzawa Hirofumi, ed., *Iryō no keizaigakuteki bunseki*, (Nippon Hyōron Sha, 1987).
Note: The figures for morbidity and treatment are as of the survey date; the mortality figures are the composite for the year.

mortality rate for the different age cohorts as of 1955, prior to the introduction of universal health insurance in Japan.

While it is important to note that the measurement of morbidity here is based not on physicians' diagnoses but on individuals' self-assessment of their physical condition at the time the survey was taken, it is significant that both morbidity and mortality go up with age. We tend to unthinkingly accept the idea that older people have a higher mortality rate and are more likely to get sick but as of 1955 the treatment rate—the percentage of the cohort seeing a doctor—was highest for the 25–35 cohort and declined with increasing age. This is not what we would expect.

With the introduction of universal health insurance in 1961, the line plotting the treatment rate rotates counterclockwise to take a positive slope,

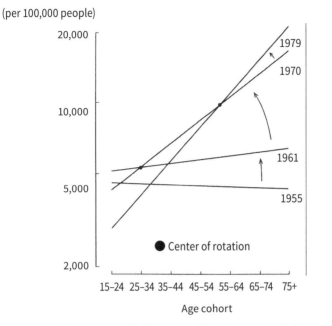

Figure 16. Semi-log graph of treatment rates by age cohort

(per 100,000 people)

1979

1970

1961

1955

● Center of rotation

15-24 25-34 35-44 45-54 55-64 65-74 75+

Age cohort

Source: Negishi Tatsuo and Naitō Masako "Genjō to sono haikei kara mita 21-seiki no iryō seido," in Uzawa Hirofumi, ed., *Iryō no keizaigakuteki bunseki*, (Nippon Hyōron Sha, 1987).

Note: The figures for morbidity and treatment are as of the survey date; the mortality figures are the composite for the year.

and the figure becomes more what we expect as normal—with treatment increasing for the older cohorts. This pattern, with older cohorts showing higher treatment rates, held throughout the rapid-growth era and beyond. This shows up clearly in Figure 16, where the 1970 treatment-rate line is very steep and the difference caused by universal health insurance is stark.

Concern started to be expressed about the burgeoning expenditures on health care in 1980 and it was argued that the treatment rate for the older cohorts was too high—that old people might be going to the doctor far more often than necessary. Even if there is an element of truth to this, I would argue that Figure 16's treatment-rate line for the rapid-growth years showing more treatment for older cohorts is a fully justifiable change for the better. Prior to the advent of universal health insurance, the treatment rate declined with age as large numbers of old people elected for economic reasons not to see a doctor. Universal health insurance is thought to have pushed up the treatment rate for seniors by alleviating this economic disincentive, and this presumably contributed to the longer life expectancies people enjoyed. We do not have the statistics needed to rigorously prove this hypothesis, but not only was average life expectancy higher after rapid growth than it had been before, there was presumably less lifespan variation among people born in the same year. It is easy to see how the higher treatment rates for the older cohorts might have been a contributory factor here.

The longer life expectancy may be counted as one of the major benefits accruing from Japan's rapid growth. Indeed, the contribution to lowering the infant mortality rate was among the greatest of rapid growth's accomplishments. In 1950, infant mortality was 6.0 percent nationwide—and nearly one in ten in the Tōhoku region. But by 1975, after rapid growth had done its work, the national average had plunged to 1.0 percent, and there had also been a major reduction in the regional disparities. This striking elimination of the heartbreak that comes from losing an infant child is something Japan can be proud of.

The Tragedy of Minamata

However, the rapid growth story is not a tale of unmitigated good alone. Japan has a long history of pollution, including the environmental disaster at the Ashio Copper Mine that Tanaka Shōzō did so much to confront in the late nineteenth and early twentieth centuries. Yet there seems to have been a quantum leap in the proliferation and severity of air pollution, water pollution, noise pollution, vibration pollution, ground subsidence, and more accompanying the postwar rapid growth. Even as the problem was growing worse and the public was growing more concerned, polluting companies and the government alike not only ignored the problem but denied its existence and covered up their culpability, thereby making the problem worse and causing untold suffering, from 1950 to 1967 when the Basic Act for Environmental Pollution Control was passed—basically the whole of the rapid-growth period. The effects are still being felt even today. It was only in May 1996—a full 40 years after the Minamata poisoning was identified—that the largest group of Minamata plaintiffs reached an agreement with Chisso (the successor to Shin-Nihon Chisso Hiryō [New Japan Nitrogenous Fertilizer])—the company responsible for dumping toxic effluent in their water, contaminating their food supply, and more.

Essentially, the Minamata disease was caused by methylmercury effluent in Minamata Bay. Abnormalities had been detected in the nervous systems of fish, cats, birds, and other animals in Minamata, Kumamoto, almost immediately after the war ended. Crows fell from the sky; cats did a nervous-twitchy dance and died. Yet it was not until 1956 that Hosokawa Hajime, director of the Chisso Minamata Plant Hospital, officially announced that he was seeing large numbers of patients with an unidentified central nervous system affliction of unknown cause. (Earlier cases have since been confirmed.)

The Kumamoto University School of Medicine formed a special Minamata research team and made an intense effort to identify the causes. In July 1959, they finally determined that it was caused by methylmercury in the effluent runoff from the Chisso Minamata plant. This finding was, however, hotly contested by the Chisso plant director and other Chisso executives, most of whom had engineering backgrounds, and they promptly released a counter-finding seeking to quash the university finding. Following up, the company continued to stubbornly maintain that its acetaldehyde production process did not yield any methylmercury.

However, even as the company was putting up a defiant front, its own in-house research very strongly suggested that plant effluent was indeed the cause of the Minamata affliction. After Minamata patients were identified, the plant hospital director, Hosokawa, did a number of animal experiments, feeding cats a diet of fish and other food exposed to factory runoff. When the results implicated methylmercury from the plant, they were contested on the grounds that the fish and food had been exposed to other effluent as well, so Hosokawa gave the cats a number of different effluent solutions as drinking water. In October 1959, cat number 400 developed Minamata symptoms after drinking effluent from the plant's acetaldehyde production process. (Over 800 cats were used in all, and they were identified by their record numbers.) The Chisso management, however, suppressed this finding, which later redounded to the company's disadvantage when the study was discovered and the plaintiffs argued that what might have been gross negligence before was knowing, willful culpability once the company was aware of the cat-400 report.

In December 1959—two months after the cat-400 finding—the company signed an out-of-court settlement providing condolence payments; this settlement also contained a stipulation that the plaintiffs would not seek any further indemnification even if the causes of the affliction were clearly ascertained. Subsequently, in a court hearing on July 20, 1972, one of the plaintiffs described the agreement process: "We were given a blank sheet of paper and told to sign it. We had no idea how much this condolence payment would be, much less that this would be considered some sort of contract." In the meantime, Chisso had doubled its acetaldehyde production, from 70 tons per day in 1958 to 140 tons per day in 1959. This too was rapid growth.

At the time, acetaldehyde was a prime ingredient in Octonol, one of Chisso's best-selling products. Even so, that is not enough to explain why Chisso's management and experts persisted in ignoring the large and growing body of evidence that plant effluent was causing the affliction, continued to argue that the production process did not generate any methylmercury, and continued to ramp up production. Were their own children suffering similarly, reasonable people would surely have moved to escape the very probable cause even if they did not have the level of proof that Chisso demanded. Yet the plant director—who was said to be a hard-working man devoted to his job and who was later (1988) found guilty by the Supreme Court of negligent homicide—had this to say in his defense on May 14, 1971: "Weighing the benefits from the plant's operation against the losses from the suffering, I could not justify stopping the plant just because someone died."

These words, honestly spoken, epitomize the corporate culture during the rapid-growth era, and such thinking dominated the Ministry of International Trade and Industry and the rest of the economy for all too long. It was not until September 1968—a full 12 years after Dr. Hosokawa had issued his report on the ailment—that the government finally agreed that Minamata disease was caused by the methylmercury effluent from the production line at the Chisso Minamata Factory and designated it pollution-caused.

Such corporate-think was not restricted to companies or to management circles. Even the unions, which had been so vociferous in opposing the productivity threat before shifting to a more conciliatory stance, lined up with employers in downplaying pollution and the idea that companies should change their ways in the broader public interest. When a group of 15 Minamata victims and the American photographer Eugene Smith (1918–1978) visited the Chisso Plant in Goi, Chiba, in 1972 to protest the company's stance, they were violently set upon by 200 of the workers there. It was not at all uncommon for union workers at polluting companies to see the people campaigning against pollution as "the enemy."

Chisso had been the driving force in producing the nitrogen that was integral to electrochemistry since well before the war, and most of the other zaibatsu-affiliated companies had left that work to Chisso and moved into petrochemicals.

Smog

Starting around 1960, there were a number of new littoral industrial complexes constructed in Kawasaki, Yokkaichi, Iwakuni, and elsewhere. I was still in junior high and high school in the 1960s and have vivid memories of how our social science textbooks portrayed these littoral industrial complexes in glowing terms. Plastics produced by the petrochemical industry transformed our lives in many ways, and life without plastics is unimaginable today. As shown earlier in Table 5, the petrochemical industry was an icon of Japan's rapid growth.

Industrial parks proliferated not only on the coasts but inland as well, all of them enthusiastically supported as engines of regional development. The general feeling was that people could not make an adequate living from farming and fishing alone, and attracting industry was seen as the way of the future. This was also the reasoning behind landfilling parts of Tokyo Bay and the Seto Inland Sea in the 1950s.

Yokkaichi was typical. Yokkaichi boasted the completion of its Petrochemical Complex No. 1 in 1959 and No. 2 in 1960, growing to account for one-fourth of Japan's petrochemical production capacity. About the same time, there was a sudden increase in severe asthma among children, old people, and other area residents. This was soon traced to the sulfurous acid gas spewing from the petrochemical complexes' smokestacks. This ailment later came to be called Yokkaichi Asthma and was infamous nationwide. Not only did it kill a number of people, the extreme suffering that it caused drove a number of others to suicide. Children went to school wearing yellow "pollution masks" containing activated charcoal. When the stench of the sulfurous acid gas was particularly bad, people kept their windows closed and turned on air purifiers. Even so, a 1967 survey of school attendance showed sixth-graders in Yokkaichi missing 2.9 times as many days of school as the national average. It was also reported (in a 1965 study at Shiohama Elementary School) that this pollution was negatively impacting the children's growth.

By the mid-1960s, rapid industrialization's downside was obvious to all.

The successful citizen campaign to block the construction of a new industrial complex in the Mishima-Numazu area in 1964 was symbolic of this turnabout in public perceptions. In a piece titled "Kieta kombināto" (The Complex That Wasn't) in the above-cited *Shōgen: Kōdo seichōki no Nihon*, vol. 1, Kumagai Yasushi, who was the prefectural official responsible for promoting the local siting of the complex, reminisced:

NHK spent some television time on the Yokkaichi pollution problem, and this was another factor leading to the spread of opposition to our proposal. That and the earthquake in Niigata that caused a fire at a petroleum tank there.

Looking back, there is a lot the prefecture could have done better. Instead, we sought to counter the protesters by distributing printed material claiming there would be zero pollution. You really should not try to fool people like that, and it is hardly credible to claim that everything is going to be a hundred percent pollution-free. . . .

Even so, looking back, the Numazu campaign against us did a truly magnificent job of mobilizing public opinion. Conservatives do not generally get on board with campaigns like this, but the Numazu people managed to involve all manner of organizations all across the spectrum. They pointed the way to a new style of citizens' campaign. It was no surprise they had the local trade union council, the teachers' union, the Socialist Party, and the Communist Party opposing us, but by the time they were done their coalition included independent doctors and teachers, women's organizations, the mayor, neighborhood organizations, and practically everyone else. There were about twenty thousand people at the September 1964 mass rally in Numazu. Even the farmers were there. The farmers from Nakazato, who were in favor of the project at first, were out there on their tillers and tractors railing against us.

We had never seen anything like it, and this opposition campaign was one for the history books.

In June 1964, the Mishima city council rejected a proposal for the construction of a new industrial complex that had the strong backing of the Ministry of International Trade and Industry and the Shizuoka prefectural government. The Niigata Minamata suit was filed in 1967, soon followed by filings in what were seen as the Big Four pollution cases (Kumamoto Minamata affliction,

Niigata Minamata affliction, Itai-itai Disease, and Yokkaichi Asthma). The Diet enacted the Basic Law for Environmental Pollution Control that same year. By 1970, a total of 14 pollution-related laws had been passed, and the Environmental Agency (upgraded to the Environmental Ministry in 2001) was established in 1971.

Such is not, however, to imply that the pollution problems have been solved. In fact, the onslaught of motorization in the late 1960s exacerbated urban pollution. After discussing the increasing number of traffic accidents, architect Nishiyama Uzō added:

> Nor are traffic accidents the only problem. The deafening noise, the air pollution that makes our urban environments unfit for human life, and more—is proper accounting being made of these negatives as well? Instead, they just talk about the additional jobs that have been created to deal with pollution, how much busier the doctors and undertakers are, and how grateful we should be that our lives have gotten so much better. (Nishiyama Uzō, "Seikatsu kakushin no vijon," in *Nishiyama Uzō cho-saku-shū*, vol. 2, *Jūkyo-ron* [Keisō Shobō, 1968])

It used to be said that corporations were the perpetrators and ordinary citizens the victims of pollution, but motorization has complicated this, and it turns out that ordinary people with their automobiles are both the causes of this pollution and its victims. The photochemical smog warnings that were issued in the summer of 1970, just as Japan's rapid growth was drawing to a close, were symbolic markers of how much worse our environmental conditions were.

Rapid economic growth contributed to lengthening Japanese life expectancy and was likely a contributory factor in narrowing the regional disparities in longevity. The same may well be said of incomes. As average incomes rose, the disparities among individuals narrowed. Yet "income" here is purely in monetary terms and takes no consideration of environmental pollution or like factors. I will return to this discussion in the next chapter.

No matter how beneficial this rapid economic growth may have been on average, the victims afflicted with serious pollution-related ailments may be forgiven for thinking we would have been better off without this economic growth. Commenting on the conclusion of the Minamata court proceedings, the historian Irokawa Daikichi wrote:

The Minamata affliction was not a price we had to pay for rapid economic growth and the resulting national affluence. Quite the reverse. The rapid growth was made possible by a social climate that ignored these horrific conditions and made the pursuit of profit its ultimate priority. (*Asahi Shimbun*, July 3, 1996, evening edition)

This is one cogent critique of Japan's rapid growth. Pollution's victims were primarily disadvantaged members of society. In 1956, nearly half of the households with people suffering from Minamata's pollution were also said to be receiving public welfare assistance. The children and old people who accounted for so many of pollution's victims are the populations at risk health-wise whatever the era.

Japan's rapid economic growth contributed to lowering the infant mortality rate and extending the average life expectancy, but it was an abject failure in terms of minimizing harm to society's most vulnerable members. Seen in that light, it is worth asking ourselves anew what exactly economic growth is and means.

CHAPTER 8

Looking Back, Summing Up

Tokyo Tower during its construction, completed in 1958.
(© Kyodo News, licensed by Tokyo Tower)

From the mid-1980s to the early 1990s, Japan's was a bubble economy. Real economic growth in 1988 was 6.7 percent, the highest recorded since the end of the rapid-growth era. Yet this growth fell off sharply in the 1990s and Japan suffered serious economic malaise, with growth figures of 1.1 percent in 1992 and minus 1.0 percent in 1993. Even though there was some modest improvement after that, the economy was beset by prolonged sluggishness, earning that era the sobriquet "the lost decade." The economic doldrums since the turn of the century would have been unimaginable during the rapid-growth years.

That said, real GNP in 1994 was 10 times what it had been in the early 1950s, which means that 1 percent growth in 1994 was equivalent in absolute GNP terms to 10 percent growth as of the first part of the 1950s. Factoring in that the population had increased about 30 percent in the interim, growth of 10 percent in the very early 1950s was comparable in per capita terms to 1.3 percent in the mid-1990s. Measured in numbers of apples, for example, it took only one-eighth as much GNP growth in the mid-1990s to provide each person the same number of additional apples as they would have gotten from 10 percent growth in the early 1950s. Yet for the growth rate to languish close to or even below zero is bound to introduce distortions in the economic structure. The dismal job market for young people is a case in point.

This brings us back to the questions of what economic growth is and why it matters. What does GNP growth mean? What is this thing called growth? If you think in terms of a growing child, proud parents often put marks on the wall and date them so they can see how tall and how fast the child has grown. Likewise with our earnings, which we track from year to year. That much is simple. Yet it gets a little more complicated when we start talking about measuring how much and how fast a country's economy has grown.

Taking things one at a time, let us look first at our measuring stick—GNP—to see just what it is measuring.

GNP's Limitations

The concept of measuring gross national product was first formulated by the British economist William Petty in the seventeenth century and then refined by later economists seeking to understand growth better. (As touched upon earlier, most economists now use not gross *national* product [GNP] but gross *domestic* product [GDP], but the differences between them need not concern us here. This book uses the two terms interchangeably.) Once accepted, the GNP concept proved invaluable to tracking the growth of the British economy as it came to dominate the global economy. At the same time, it promised to provide a convenient measure of how much wealth was accruing to the working class under capitalism, a question of major concern to economists at the time. Somewhat of a latecomer, Japan did not adopt GNP as a statistical standard until the early twentieth century. After considerable discussion and debate, the indicator reached very much its current form in the late nineteenth and early twentieth centuries. Even then, the GNP concept was—and still is—subject to tweaks and refinements from a wide range of economists, even after the United Nations adopted a standard definition in the wake of World War II.

From the very start, it was hoped that GNP would do more than just measure the size of the nation's economy and would also be a measure of national welfare, or what might be termed a happiness index. Of course, the economists who initially developed it were very cautious on this point. Writing in his seminal 1920 work, *The Economics of Welfare*, University of Cambridge Professor Arthur Pigou noted that welfare has both economic and non-economic aspects and that it would be beneficial overall to enhance the economic aspects if the two are independent of each other, but that it sometimes happens that enhancing the economic aspects has a negative impact on the non-economic aspects, or externalities. Although Pigou himself did not use the term GNP, he was at great pains to explain how and why the economics alone were insufficient to understanding wealth. There was and is a major disparity between GNP and personal wealth or happiness.

That said, GNP was emblematic of the Japanese economy's—and hence Japan's—development in the rapid-growth era. Who could have forecast in the early 1950s that Japan's GNP would overtake the figures for the United

Kingdom and France? Yet it did, and this achievement was immensely satisfying to the Japanese citizenry. But going into the latter half of the 1960s, the collateral damage associated with growth became painfully evident, and people's pride of accomplishment turned to concern for the future. Particularly noteworthy here was the 18-part column in the *Asahi Shimbun* in 1970 titled "Kutabare GNP" (Fuck GNP). This headline phrase trended heavily as the column expounded from a variety of angles on just how divorced GNP is from any sense of personal wealth and happiness.

Why is GNP so unsuited to measuring personal affluence? Very simply, GNP is by definition a measure of aggregate monetary transactions and hence includes any and all monetary transactions as positives, even if they are irrelevant or even detrimental to any sense of enrichment. Likewise, it fails to account for non-monetized activity such as the tremendous effort that parents expend on raising their children (which would, however, be included if they outsourced this and paid someone else to make the same effort). While some people have tried to cite GNP as a measure of personal enrichment, their explanations have always come up short.

There is no end to examples of the folly of equating GNP with personal happiness. If there is an influenza epidemic that pushes up demand for medical services, the increased income accruing to medical professionals counted as a plus for GNP. The same with traffic accidents—and the mind-boggling legal fees in a litigious society such as the United States. Indeed, it seems the more trouble and strife there is in society, the higher the GNP. Having to spend a lot of money commuting to work may be good for GNP, but it is hard to see how it enriches our lives. Indeed, many of these things impoverish our lives. Back when over half of the Japanese people lived and worked in rural villages, their commuting costs were essentially nil. As industrialization and urbanization progressed in tandem with rapid economic growth, people lived farther from their workplaces, commuting expenses went up, and GNP also went up—but at what cost?

Pollution is another example. Despite the obvious fact that pollution has negatively impacted our lives, it is a negative externality and, not being a monetary transaction, is not reflected in GNP figures. Yet if the pollution is so bad as to require remedial measures, these measures—no matter if they are inadequate and do little or nothing to improve the quality of our lives—are accounted in monetary terms and included to boost GNP while the negative externalities continue to be ignored.

Even looking at the few examples cited here—and there are many more that could have been cited—leads to the questions: What is GNP anyway, and isn't there something better we could use? In an effort to answer the second question, the Kingdom of Bhutan has developed what it calls its Gross National Happiness (GNH) index, which has drawn considerable attention internationally. Recognizing that GNP is not entirely useless, efforts are also being made to amend it to better reflect real living standards. There is, for example, the Measures of Economic Welfare (MEW) which the economists James Tobin and William Nordhaus proposed in an attempt to take the aforementioned parental efforts (positive) and pollution (negative) into account. Close on its heels was Net National Welfare (NNW), proposed in 1973. In all of this, economists have noted that US economic growth from 1929 to 1965 averages out to 1.7 percent per annum if calculated in GNP terms but only 1.1 percent in MEW terms and have pointed out that compensating for GNP's systemic shortcomings does not radically change the GNP ballpark figure for economic growth. As such, it seems reasonable to conclude that, while GNP is seriously flawed as a measure of economic welfare, it is not meaningless in and of itself. Does this then mean that GNP growth, or more generally modern economic growth, is a good thing?

The Modernization Paradigm

In *The Stages of Economic Growth* (1959), Walt Rostow offered an unequivocal "yes" in answer to this question. Rostow postulated five easy-to-understand stages that he said characterized all economic development patterns everywhere: traditional society, preconditions to take-off, take-off, drive to maturity, and an age of high mass consumption. This thesis was not without its critics, and heated debate ensued. Much of the debate centered on what Rostow called the take-off stage—which was akin to the industrial revolution stage, itself a much-disputed concept today—and this became both the centerpiece of Rostow's thesis and a major focus in discussing developing countries' development process. However, this is not the place to go into detail on that, since our concern here is more with his age of high mass consumption.

Rostow asserted that the high mass consumption society—a term that has since become commonplace—is the goal to which all economies, the United States foremost among them, should and do aspire. Following up, he cites the advances of the golden-age 1920s and the first decade after World War II as having made the United States a high mass consumption society. A bit later, he says, the West European countries and Japan also embarked firmly on the path to becoming high mass consumption societies in the 1950s. Such was Rostow's thinking as of the late 1950s.

It would be easy enough to poke holes in Rostow's linear view of history and his rather arbitrary demarcation of the stages of development, and there were indeed many people who characterized his modernization theory—his assumption that history is necessarily a story of progress—as overly simplistic. However, the subsequent collapse of the socialist states, the path of development followed by the Four Dragons (South Korea, Taiwan, Hong Kong, and Singapore), the rapid economic growth achieved by China, India, Brazil, and the like, and other developments that followed make it impossible to discount Rostow's developmental theories entirely.

Likewise, there can be no question but that Japan's own rapid-growth process was clearly based on seeking to become a high mass consumption society. Prime among the criteria that Rostow postulated in defining the high mass consumption society was the proliferation of consumer durables, especially automobiles. Rebounding from the war, Japan quickly jumped aboard the Rapid Growth Super-Express bound for an American lifestyle luxuriating in consumer durables, in the belief that attaining this lifestyle would vastly enrich all of our lives.

Looking back at the changes engendered during this period lends considerable credibility to Rostow's discourse. It is impossible to negate the convenience offered by the new washing machines, refrigerators, and other appliances, which is why even today developing countries are in hot pursuit of modernization and the material wealth it promises. What is happening in next-door China provides all the further explanation anyone could want.

Very broadly speaking, modernization is the process of moving from an agrarian society to an industrial society and upgrading the makeup of the industrial sector with technological innovation, the energy revolution, and other advances to achieve major productivity gains. After all, who would object to growing the apple pie if it became possible for each person to get not 365 apples but 730 apples? This is the growth-affirming logic of modernization. Seen in this way, it is virtually impossible to oppose modernization's economic growth—what might be called GNP growth, albeit with GNP suitably modified to compensate for the pollution and other negative externalities that accompany this growth. Even so, the question remains: Is it really that simple?

Is Bigger Better?

It has long been believed that modernization and the accompanying economic growth constitute Progress with a capital P. Back to our apples, going from 365 apples to 730 apples is the very definition of progress. That is the theory. Yet the actual experience with rapid growth is that it permeates and fundamentally alters every nook and cranny of our lives—even the sensibilities of people caught up in it—and not always for the better. Along the way, it has also powered many negative changes and has caused us to lose sight of all of those precious things, large and small, that are not amenable to valuation in monetary terms. It is beyond human imagining how great the cost of environmental degradation worldwide has been. Further, the marketplace has no room for the sensitivity and empathy needed to understand and deal with the trauma suffered by young teenagers torn from their villages and shipped out on the midnight train to unfamiliar labor among strangers in unfamiliar settings. Natsume Sōseki famously gave an address in Wakayama in 1911 titled "Gendai Nihon no kaika" (The Civilization of Modern-Day Japan). In it, he explained the "civilization" that is the fruit of modern economic growth:

> We have these two intertwining processes: one involving inventions and mechanisms that spring from the desire to conserve our labor as much as possible, and the other involving amusements that spring from the wish to consume our energies as freely as possible. As these two intertwine like a textile's warp and woof, combining in infinitely varied ways, the result is this strange, chaotic phenomenon we know as our modern civilization. (From the translation by Jay Rubin in Natsume Sōseki, *Kokoro: A Novel and Selected Essays*, trans. Edwin McClellan and Jay Rubin [The Library of Japan edition, 1992])

It is currently estimated that Japanese real GNP doubled in the quarter-century up to 1911, when Sōseki gave his talk. Sōseki would have had full opportunity to experience the many conveniences ensuing from the nation's opening. Yet he continued:

> I said earlier that, for all its progress, civilization favors us with so little peace of mind that, if we consider the added anxieties thrust upon us by competition and the like, our happiness is probably not very different from what it was in the stone age.

To this indictment, he added that Japan's civilization,

> is not internally, but externally motivated. This tells us that the civiliza-
> tion of modern-day Japan is superficial: it just skims the surface.... This
> is not to say we must put a stop to it. There is really nothing we can do
> about it. We must go on skimming the surface, fighting back our tears.

Forty years after Sōseki issued his indictment, Japan embarked upon its
postwar rapid growth—rapid growth that profoundly transformed Japanese
society in a mere 6,000 days. Looking back, can we really say with full confidence that this transformation was Progress and A Good Thing?

Afterword to the 1997 Hardcover Edition

There are two reasons I decided to ignore the fact that I am not a historian by profession and write this book. First is that it is very much about economics, which is my profession. In looking at economic growth and seeking to explain it, economists typically draw upon mathematical models. Yet I have long felt that such models leave out too much of the really important parts. As John Hicks—one of the leading economists of the twentieth century—has said, economists seeking to analyze the growth phenomenon should do so with as much of the historian's mindset as possible. I think he is right, and I wanted to try to do this—to get away from the mathematical models and bring a historian's approach to the discussion of Japan's postwar growth.

My second reason is somewhat more personal. Born in 1951, I spent basically the whole of my school years in the rapid-growth era. I went from kindergarten to university in the rapid-growth whirlwind, and I wanted a chance to look back on those years and what they meant for everybody. The result is this book. It is a somewhat personal retrospective, but I hope it provides a useful reference for readers who are themselves interested in looking back on what happened and what it all meant.

Although the end result is a somewhat modest book, it benefited greatly from the generous assistance offered by so many people. Among the people heading but by no means exhausting the list are Fujisawa Atsuko, Atsuya Tsukasa, Tomii Hitomi, Tsugawa Shinako, and Nishida Maki of the University of Tokyo Faculty of Economics Office; Tsumura Hisako and Takahara Junko of the University of Tokyo Computer Services Office; and Hosoya Miho for her help when she was a junior at Tokyo Women's Christian University. Outside of academia, I am also indebted to Yomiuri Shimbun Publishing's Kataya Katsumi and Kawahito Ken'ichi for supporting the publication of this book so wholeheartedly. Both of these gentlemen came to my office at the university numerous times during the tumult of the communications revolution, and I have fond memories of talking with them.

And finally is my wife Setsuko, who not only put up with me but found time in her own busy schedule to read over the manuscript and provide many invaluable comments and suggestions. To all of these people, I am sincerely and immensely grateful.

Yoshikawa Hiroshi
February 26, 1997

Afterword to the 2012 Paperback Edition

My *Kōdō seichō: Nihon o kaeta 6,000 nichi* (Rapid Growth: The 6,000 Days that Transformed Japan) was originally published in 1997 as one of the books in the Japan in the Twentieth Century series issued to commemorate the Yomiuri Shimbun's 120th anniversary. As the title suggests, it was written to discuss the many economic and social changes that took place in Japan in the rapid-growth years from the mid-1950s to 1970. This rapid-growth era was a mere 6,000 days, yet it radically transformed Japan—a transformation so profound that it deserves to be classified as a period in its own right, alongside the Heian period and the Kamakura period. Indeed, historians will long be debating what, exactly, this rapid growth was and meant for Japan.

We are already so well past the rapid-growth era that it feels like ancient history. Yet economic growth continues to be an important social and economic issue for Japan. Thus it is that the book is being reissued as a paperback, and I am taking this opportunity to append an afterword questioning the economic growth mantra.

When the book was first published in 1997, Kanamori Hisao kindly reviewed it in the weekly *Ekonomisuto* (July 1, 1997). Not only had Kanamori supervised the writing of the Economic Planning Agency's economic white papers in the midst of the rapid growth, he was an outstanding government official who had taken part in numerous debates and decisions that will be remembered when Japan's postwar economic history is written. It was thus a great honor to have him write a review of my book—especially since it turned out generally favorable.

Kanamori ended his review with these words:

> Yoshikawa concludes his book with an afterword in which he asks what this economic growth was all about, cites the environmental degradation and psychological changes that it wrought, and questions whether we can confidently assert that this rapid growth was progress. Of course

it was major progress for Japan, and I wish the author had not ended his good book on such a maddeningly irresolute note.

A government economist who was active during the rapid-growth period, Kanamori is unequivocal in stating, "Of course it was major progress for Japan." I was born in 1951 and experienced the same years as a student, starting in kindergarten and going all the way through high school. I remember taking the day off from school in 1964 (my first year of junior high) and going to see the Tokyo Olympics opening ceremony with a ticket my father had somehow procured. And I remember feeling intensely, not just then but throughout the era, that Japan's economic growth represented real progress.

Yet I wrote this book not as a teenager but as a man in his late forties who harbored an unshakable ambivalence about the economic growth story. Natsume Sōseki's "The Civilization of Modern-Day Japan," which I quoted near the end of Chapter 8, appealed to my sensitivities, and the intervening years have not changed my mind on this. That said, I am not anti-growth. Far from it. I feel economic growth is essential if we are to overcome our current boxed-in mood. This last section on rethinking growth has been appended by way of explanation.

Serious questions were already being raised about the growth-is-good axiom 40 years ago, just as Japan's rapid-growth era was drawing to a close. Specifically, the Club of Rome's 1972 *The Limits to Growth* questioning economic growth in light of the earth's finite carrying capacity marked a significant turning point in our consciousness. In the ensuing years, a growing number of people have come to feel that economic growth and economic activity itself is—if you will allow a bit of hyperbole—somehow a dirty undertaking best avoided. The very words "market fundamentalism" evoke a social mechanism entirely devoid of any human feelings, recall memories of the countless accidents that happened because management was focused solely on economic efficiency and cared nothing for human lives, and remind us of the tens of millions of innocent people worldwide who were thrown out of work when "the greedy capitalists" caused both the asset bubble and its subsequent implosion. For these people, "economic growth" is the symbol and standard bearer for the kind of capital-is-all thinking that should be consigned to the dustbin of history. Saeki Keishi, professor of economics at Kyoto University, spoke for many Japanese when he wrote in the December 17, 2011, *Yomiuri Shimbun*, "The fickle forces of nature have inflicted deep wounds on the Japanese psyche and caused innumerable people to fundamentally alter their views on life and death and on nature itself. Japan's postwar values system that argued expanding production would bring wealth and freedom and Japan's very concept of happiness have both crumbled in the onslaught of collateral damage."

This is not something unique to the late twentieth and early twenty-first centuries. The new-wave romanticism that arose in Europe in the early nineteenth century was itself a reaction (antithesis) to the emergence of capitalism. In fact, such sentiments can be seen widely around the world and throughout history. Indeed, history may well be seen as a constant conflicting intermix of romanticism turning its back on economic concerns and rationalism critical of such romanticism.

Laozi (Lao Tzu), for example, may be seen as anti-growth and anti-economics with his "artless life" admonition to "consider the food before you delicious, the clothes on your back beautiful, and your pleasures enjoyable" —essentially to accept life as it comes and be satisfied with your lot, knowing that we are part of nature. Little wonder there are many who seem to feel that this whole idea of seeking economic growth is a Western contrivance at odds with the Oriental philosophy that he espoused.

While it can be argued that Eastern and Western values are fundamentally different and divergent, such is not the whole story, as illustrated by the fact that Laozi's "thou shalt not covet" philosophy was harshly criticized by Confucianism, said to be the very pinnacle of Eastern thinking. Han Yu, for example, ranks alongside Liu Zongyuan as one of the most esteemed writers of the Tang dynasty and his *Yuan Dao* is an era-defining work. In it, he writes that "many were the plagues on man in olden times" by way of stating that the environment was indeed harsh when the ancients lived and that those people who managed to achieve tangible improvements—the men who created clothing when it was cold, who provided food when hunger preyed, and who devised medicines to stave off needless death—were indeed sages. Naitō Konan (pen name of Naitō Torajirō, 1866–1934), one of the most respected scholars of Oriental history, thus wrote in his *Zōtei Nihon bunkashi kenkyū* (Research on Japanese Cultural History, expanded edition [Kōbundō, 1930], 67), "The Chinese term for people who make things—who use their lives to devise all manner of useful tools and implements and by extension create the prototypes for our material civilization—is 'sage,' and in that sense this encompasses everyone from Fuxi and Shennong down through King

Wen and King Wu of Zhou and Zhougong [the Duke of Zhou]." A sage in Confucian thought is thus equivalent to an innovator—one who performs the innovation that Schumpeter says is the essential driver of capitalism.

Looking at society today, we find some resistance to modernization and its emphasis on life's economic aspects, but how many who espouse such views would refuse modern antibiotics if they fell ill? While the Isewan Typhoon left over 5,000 people dead or missing in 1959, the number of deaths from typhoons is far lower today. Surely we should acknowledge this as one of the blessings of modern civilization. Laozi's philosophy is impractical in practice. Such is Han Yu's perception. Some may deride Han Yu as an ancient relic, but he espouses a realism that stands in sharp contrast to and is fundamentally at odds with Laozi. Together, Han Yu's Confucianism and the Zhu Xi brand of neo-Confucianism that informed the ruling class for the Edo period's two and a half centuries (1603–1868) show Confucianism clearly favoring attention to economic concerns and capitalism.

I am not, of course, invoking Confucianism here to convince anyone of economic growth's primacy. With the increasing concern over global sustainability, I doubt there is anyone who would advocate unfettered growthism and see economic growth as an end in and of itself. Rather, there is the opposite danger that some will forget the benefits growth has brought us and adopt an unthinking anti-growth line. There are, for example, those who, seeing only part of the picture, glorify the Edo period as a slow-growth, sustainable social model. While I readily admit there was much to admire in Edo society, I think we must also acknowledge the negative elements. In this connection, I was struck by an article titled "Hone ga kataru Edo jijō" (What the Bones Tell Us about Edo Life) that appeared in the evening edition of the *Asahi Shimbun* on December 27, 2011. It reported:

> The National Museum of Nature and Science has a very large collection of bones unearthed in excavating for development projects in Tokyo. . . . They tell us much about life in the Edo period. Nutrition was poor and especially iron-deficient. It is also noteworthy that there are many bones of young people—many more than you would expect given the low mortality rate for people that age today. Epidemics were frequent and death was commonplace.
>
> Average adult height was in the 150–60 centimeter range for males, with females about 10 centimeters shorter. This is the smallest Japanese

have ever been in any era. Not only was nutrition bad, there was considerable stress from having to live crowded together in small row houses. Forensic anthropologist Shinoda Ken'ichi has commented, "Life was hard, and these bones are eloquent testimony to the darker side of life in what might be called the slum that was Edo."

The conventional wisdom among economists is that economics and population were closely linked in the Edo period. It was during this period that Robert Malthus wrote his seminal *An Essay on the Principle of Population* (1798). Malthus and other economists at the time believed that propagation of the species was instinctive to humankind and that people would behave so as to leave the largest number of progeny possible so long as food and the other means of life were available, with the result that incomes would forever be held at the lowest level that allowed subsistence. In fact, this is what prevailed in Edo, and this is the story of most people's lives in agricultural societies throughout history.

It was the Industrial Revolution and the industrialized countries' economic growth that broke this link between economic subsistence and population. Rapid economic growth was marked by the shift from being an agrarian state to being an industrial state and by spectacular increases in per capita income levels—a leap so great as to be a historic singularity. For Japan, this took place from the 1950s into the 1970s. China's time is now.

The shift from a predominately traditional society and agrarian economy to modern economic growth powered by industrialization also triggers major changes in the nation's demographics. Conspicuously, economic growth has not fed the kind of population growth that Malthus and other economists of his time forecast. Rather, it has raised income levels and lengthened life expectancies. In 1950, shortly before the rapid-growth era, Japanese life expectancy was 58.0 for males and 61.5 for females. These numbers put Japan at the bottom of the table for industrial countries. Two decades later when the rapid-growth era drew to a close in 1970, the equivalent numbers were 69.3 for males and 74.7 for females. Now, with the Japanese economy having continued to grow for another four decades, Japanese life expectancies are 80 for males and 86 for females, placing Japan at the top of the table of industrial countries. At the same time, while it may be argued that it is animal instinct to seek to leave as many progeny as possible, it may better be said, at least for the human animal, that the more important instinct is to seek to live as long as possible.

Different people look back on the rapid-growth era differently. As I mentioned in my concluding chapter, I myself am ambivalent. Yet my misgivings aside, and as someone who grew up on the rapid-growth whirlwind, I would like to offer the era a huge bouquet of flowers in appreciation.

At the same time, I would like to express my gratitude to two young people who contributed invaluably: Matsumoto Kayoko of the Chūōkōron Shinsha Liberal Arts Editorial Division for having done so much to make the publication of this paperback edition possible and Yasuda Yōsuke, one of the rising stars of the Japanese economics profession, for having generously made time to write a special commentary for inclusion.

Yoshikawa Hiroshi
March 30, 2012

Commentary
Bringing the Rapid-Growth Era to Life

This work is a retrospective by one of Japan's foremost macroeconomists ana-lyzing the rapid-growth era from a number of angles. Yet for its many readers like myself who are too young to have actually experienced that period, the first question is what this "rapid-growth era" actually means. For us, it is an unfamiliar term and unfamiliar territory. What was this rapid growth that propelled Japan from a desolate wasteland devastated by war into the world's second-largest economic power, all in the space of less than two decades once it got its postwar footing? What kind of an era was it? There is no better way to answer this and provide the setting for the Japanese miracle than to look at the book itself.

About half a century ago, Japan achieved mind-boggling economic growth. In less than 20 years, from the mid-1950s to the beginning of the 1970s, Japan's per annum economic growth was an unprecedented 10 percent. This astonishing expansion enabled the economy to double in size in a mere seven years. "In the three years from 1966 through 1968, Japan surpassed the UK, France, and West Germany, one a year, to become the second-largest Western economy (trailing only the United States) and an economic power in its own right."

This rapid growth did more than simply expand the economy. As the author notes, "All of the things that we take for granted about society and the economy—all of the assumptions that define today's Japanese—were basi-cally structured and put in place during those earlier years. Indeed, it is no exaggeration to say that the rapid growth years altered the very foundations of the Japanese state." As he also writes, "The changes that took place in a mere 6,000 days between 1955 and 1970 were far more wide-reaching and far more significant than anything that has happened in the 40 years since then." The rapid-growth experience totally revolutionized Japanese life and brought about fundamental change.

How does Yoshikawa, a macroeconomist who lived through this tumultuous era, explain the rapid growth that altered Japan's destiny? As expected, with abundant data-based macroeconomic empirical analysis and theoretical analysis of the factors that underpinned this growth. His analytical abilities as a prominent economist are on full display in this engrossing work. Yet the real attraction of this work is his many depictions of era events from a human perspective and the way he deftly evokes the lives of the people and the emotional currents involved. More than statistics, this is a book enriched with street-scene photographs as well as references to advertising, manga, and such popular print media as *Heibon Punch*, which I must admit was an unexpected but welcome side of my mentor, and by showing us how the era was reflected in these familiar everyday media he nicely supplements the macroeconomic discussion with microeconomic reality. It is a good mix that works well. As you read along, you will unconsciously be drawn into the era's ambience.

Having characterized the author as a macroeconomist, I would like to provide a bit more on his academic background. Yoshikawa is, of course, well known as a major figure in Keynesian economics. As an undergraduate, he studied under Uzawa Hirofumi at the University of Tokyo, and he did his graduate work with James Tobin at Yale. Uzawa and Tobin were the leading Keynesian economists in Japan and the US, and Yoshikawa himself has unhesitatingly acknowledged doing his research from a Keynesian perspective. As such, he has taken a consistently critical position on the neoclassicism that has (at least in academia) come to dominate macroeconomics since the 1970s or so. He has been particularly critical of the "real business cycle" theory that has been the driving force behind so much of neoclassical economics, and I vividly recall even now his emphatic dismissal of this as "nonsense."

That said, a bit of explanation is in order here, since there may be many readers who are not current on this academic infighting. John Maynard Keynes, the founder of Keynesian economics, said that understanding macroeconomic phenomena required macro thinking distinct from traditional concepts like supply and demand. Thus was born the field of macroeconomics. By contrast, advocates of the neoclassical or real business cycle theory emphasize "microfoundations"—the microlevel decisions by individual economic actors that they say underlie and account for the overall behavior of the macroeconomy. As a result, they say, the microfoundations based upon the economic actors' optimization behavior are an indispensable part of modern macroeconomic models. Yet Yoshikawa has spent decades warning of the vulnerabilities embodied in these microfoundations that look so elegant in theory and of the harm this approach does in slighting representations of reality. (Tellingly, there seems to have been a quiet upsurge in the number of economists calling themselves Keynesians in the wake of the Lehman Brothers collapse and ensuing financial crisis of 2007–08.)

I will not go into the pros and cons of these microeconomic foundations, both because of space limitations and because macroeconomic theory is not my field, but I do wonder if the author's deft depiction of economic behavior at the micro level and his breathtaking fusion of this with macroeconomic analysis might not also be revealing the real aspects that real business cycle theory fails to take into consideration and the microeconomic behavior that microfoundations miss. Perhaps I am reading too much into this, but that is how the author's depiction of the mood during the rapid-growth era draws me in.

I very much hope everyone reading this book—especially younger people—will come away with a feel for the mixture of euphoria and anxiety that prevailed during the rapid-growth years. And I suspect that the experiences portrayed herein might possibly hint at how we can break out of the boxed-in, bleak-future malaise that has afflicted Japan all these many years since the asset bubble burst in the very early 1990s.

Yasuda Yōsuke
Assistant Professor
National Graduate Institute for
  Policy Studies (GRIPS)
January 2012

Selected Bibliography

Note: The original Japanese edition has a multipage bibliography mainly of works in Japanese; this list shows only those available in English.

Cabinet Office. Economic White Paper. Published annually in Japanese since 1947; compiled by the Economic Planning Agency from 1954 to 2000.

Gordon, Andrew, ed. *Postwar Japan as History*. University of California Press, 1993.

Harada Masazumi. *Minamata Disease*. Translated by Tsushima Sachie and Timothy S. George. Kumamoto Nichinichi Shimbun Culture & Information Center, 2004.

Johanson, S. R., and C. Mosk. "Exposure, Resistance and Life Expectancy: Disease and Death during the Economic Development of Japan, 1900–1960." *Population Studies*, 1987.

Kimura Ihei. *Shōwa o utsusu* [The Shōwa Era in Pictures]. Chikuma Shobō, 1995. This four-volume work is in Japanese but features photographs that need no translation.

Komiya Ryūtarō, ed. *Postwar Economic Growth in Japan*. Translated by Robert Ozaki. University of California Press, 1966.

Kōsai Yutaka. *The Era of High-Speed Growth: Notes on the Postwar Japanese Economy*. Translated by Jacqueline Kaminski. University of Tokyo Press, 1986.

Kōsai Yutaka and Teranishi Jūrō, eds. *The Japanese Experience of Economic Reforms*. Palgrave Macmillan, 1993.

Lynn, Leonard H. *How Japan Innovates: A Comparison with the U.S. in the Case of Oxygen Steelmaking*. Westview Press, 1982.

Morita Akio et al. *Made in Japan*. E. P. Dutton, 1986.

Nakamura Takafusa. *A History of Showa Japan*. Translated by Edwin Whenmouth. University of Tokyo Press, 1998.

Nakamura Takafusa. *The Postwar Japanese Economy: Its Development and Structure, 1937–1994*. University of Tokyo Press, 1981.

Ōkawa Kazushi, ed. *Estimates of Long-Term Economic Statistics of Japan since 1868: National Income*. Tōyō Keizai Shinpō, 1966.

Ōkawa Kazushi and Henry Rosovsky. *Japanese Economic Growth: Trend Acceleration In the Twentieth Century*. Stanford University Press, 1973.

Rostow, W. W. *The Stages of Economic Growth: A Non-Communist Manifesto*. Cambridge University Press, 1991.

Shimomura Osamu. *Basic Problems of Economic Growth Policy*. Indian Statistical Institute, 1961.

Smith, Eugene. *Minamata: The Story of the Poisoning of a City, and of the People Who Choose to Carry the Burden of Courage*. Holt, Rinehart, and Winston, 1975.

Tanaka Kakuei. *Building a New Japan*. Simul Press, 1973.

Yoshikawa Hiroshi. *Macroeconomics and the Japanese Economy*. Oxford University Press, 1996.

Timeline

1945		War ends
Aug.	15	Japan surrenders; national wealth losses estimated at 49.7 billion yen by the end of August.
Sept.	—	SCAP (Allied Occupation headquarters) orders a halt to all military production, promotes the production of civilian goods, and bans overseas trade.
Nov.	6	SCAP orders the breakup of zaibatsu.
	22	Cabinet approves the agrarian land reform plan promulgating a new agrarian land-adjustment law on Dec. 29).
Dec.	22	Labor Union Act enacted.
Of note	♪	"Ringo no uta"
1946		Postwar purge conducted; new Constitution promulgated
Feb.	17	Ordinance on emergency monetary measures provides for the issuance of new yen currency, freezing old yen savings accounts, and limiting the amount of money in circulation.
Mar.	3	Price Control Ordinance
May	7	Sony established (as Tōkyō Tsūshin Kōgyō; name changed in Jan. 1958).
	19	Mass demonstrations protesting rice rationing (Food May Day).
Aug.	12	Economic Stabilization Board and Price Agency established.
Oct.	8	Reconstruction Finance Bank Act (RFB) established Jan. 25, 1947; reconstruction efforts spark inflation
Nov.	12	Wealth tax law
Dec.	27	Fourth-quarter production plan approved, with the priority production system emphasizing coal and steel.
Of note		Black markets; homeless children fill Ueno Station; strikes by coal miners and electrical power company workers; Nankai earthquake; ♪ "Kanashiki takebue."
1947		New Constitution goes into force
Jan.	31	SCAP bans general strike scheduled for Feb. 1.
Feb.	18	Clifford Strike report on reparations recommends leaving Japan enough that it can support itself.
Mar.	12	Truman Doctrine (containment strategy) announced.
Apr.	7	Labor Standards Act
Oct.	—	Toyota begins production of its Toyopet SA-model passenger car.
Dec.	22	Amended Civil Code (eliminating the *ie* and *katoku* [family] systems)
Of note		Typhoon Kathleen; ♪ "Hoshi no nagare ni"; ♪ "Naku na kobato yo"; "*Setting Sun* people"; first economic white paper (showing the government, industry, and households all running in the red).
1948		Berlin Blockade
May	17	Economic Reconstruction Board issues outline of draft for first five-year plan.
	18	Johnston Report radically reduces reparations and promotes reconstruction.
Sept.	23	Honda established.
Dec.	18	Nine principles for economic stabilization announced.

Note: Except as otherwise noted, laws, acts, ordinances, and the like are listed on the date of promulgation.

Of note		Teigin case; Shōwa Denkō case; Fukui earthquake; ♪ "Ikoku no oka"; economic white paper calls it a year to seriously rebuild the economy on a peacetime footing.
1949		**People's Republic of China established**
Mar.	7	Joseph Dodge arrives to advise on economic policy and soon submits his stabilization proposals ("Dodge Line").
Apr.	23	SCAP fixes the exchange rate at 360 yen to the dollar.
May	25	Ministry of International Trade and Industry (MITI) established; Ministry of Commerce and Industry, Trade Agency, and Coal Agency abolished.
June	1	Japan National Railways (JNR) and Japan Tobacco and Salt Monopoly Corporation established.
Sept.	15	SCAP releases full text of Shoup Mission's initial report on Japanese taxation.
Oct.	28	SCAP authorizes private company involvement in trade (as of Dec. 1 for exports, Jan. 1, 1950, for imports).
Of note		Shimoyama case; first New Year's postcards issued with prize-drawing numbers; ♪ "Nagasaki no kane"; economic white paper cites signs of stability and economic independence.
1950		**Start of Korean War**
Jan.	7	1,000 yen bills issued as new top denomination (featuring Prince Shōtoku).
May	26	Comprehensive National Land Development Act
July	1	Steel controls abolished (subsidies for steel materials abolished and pig iron subsidies halved).
	11	General Council of Trade Unions of Japan (Sōhyō) formed.
	—	Sony puts Japan's first tape recorder on the market.
Aug.	24	Cabinet approves price control policy to curtail price gouging taking advantage of the boom in procurements related to the Korean War.
Oct.	7	Dodge revisits Japan and calls for maintenance of anti-inflation policies and improvements in fiscal management.
	23	Textile industry equipment caps lifted.
Nov.	10	NHK starts testing television broadcasts.
	11	Kurashiki Rayon (Kuraray) begins production of Vinylon.
Of note		Typhoon Jane; Red Purge; National Police Reserve established; economic white paper focuses on the Japanese economy under stabilization planning.
1951		**MacArthur leaves Japan**
Mar.	31	Japan Development Bank Law (RFB dissolved Jan. 16, 1952)
Apr.	5	SCAP releases the Marquat report on the transfer of economic policy authority.
	12	Tōyō Rayon (Toray) receives approval to use DuPont nylon production technology.
	12	Kyōwa Hakkō Kōgyō and Meiji Seika receive approval to use Merck streptomycin production technology.
May	1	Electrical power industry reorganized into nine regional power companies.
July	18	Kōbe Kōgyō licenses television technology from RCA; 38 other companies follow suit.
	31	Japan Airlines (JAL) established, starts flights connecting Tokyo, Osaka, and Fukuoka on Oct. 25.
Sept.	8	San Francisco Peace Treaty and US-Japan Security Treaty signed.

Of note		Yakai case; Rikidōzan begins professional wrestling career; economic white paper cites issues in achieving economic independence; average life expectancy tops 60.
1952		San Francisco Peace Treaty takes effect
Jan.	16	Government announces five-year plan to develop electrical power industry (Electric Power Development Promotion Act promulgated July 31).
Mar.	14	Enterprise Rationalization Promotion Act
	—	Honda launches "Cub" moped.
Apr.	28	San Francisco Peace Treaty takes effect (SCAP abolished and foreign currency controls revert to Japan).
May	7	Ordinance prohibiting use of zaibatsu trade names voided, paving the way for the rebirth of Mitsubishi Bank, Sumitomo Bank, and the like.
	29	Japan admitted to International Monetary Fund and World Bank.
June	—	Act on Special Measures Concerning Road Construction and Improvement; Amended Road Act
Dec.	23	Nissan Motors gains approval to access Austin Motor (UK) technology.
Of note		JAL "Jupiter" plane crash; May Day incident; Suita case; see-through nylon blouses popular; pachinko boom; Shirai Yoshio wins world flyweight title; ♪ "Ringo oiwake"; ♪ "Tennessee Waltz"; economic white paper discusses Japan's ability to stand alone economically.
1953		End of Korean War
Feb.	1	NHK starts broadcasting regularly scheduled television broadcasts in Tokyo region.
Mar.	23	First group of people repatriated from China aboard the *Kōan-maru* and the *Takasago-maru* (repatriation from the Soviet Union starts in December).
June	26	US and Japan exchange notes on Mutual Security Act assistance.
July	1	Japan admitted to International Civil Aviation Organization.
Aug.	28	Nippon Television launches first commercial television broadcasts (stimulating the popularity of outdoor television showings).
	—	Sanyo launches first pulsator-type washing machine.
Oct.	13	Electric Power Development Coordination Council adopts five-year plan for electrical power.
Of note		Protests over Uchinada firing range; Dior craze; first supermarket opens; jazz popularized; economic white paper considers the preconditions to achieving economic independence.
1954		
Jan.	20	Tokyo Metro Marunouchi subway line opens between Ikebukuro and Ochanomizu (first new subway line since WWII).
Feb.	2	JAL starts flying between Tokyo and San Francisco (first regularly scheduled international flights by Japanese carrier).
	2	Sony receives approval to license US transistor technology.
July	1	Defense Agency and Ground, Maritime, and Air Self-Defense Forces established.
Dec.	10	First Hatoyama Ichirō cabinet takes office.
Of note		Shipbuilding contract scandal; *Tōya-maru* accident; law passed mandating school lunch programs; professional wrestling popularity soars; start of Jinmu Boom (lasting until early 1957); economic white paper says it is a time of consolidating the foundations for sustainable growth and development.

1955		1955 political structure coalesces.
Jan.	7	Toyota announces its Toyopet Crown line.
	28	Six industry-wide labor unions (including at private railway companies) join forces to demand wage hikes (start of *shuntō* [spring labor offensive] tradition).
Mar.	—	Japan Productivity Center established (without Sōhyō participation).
Apr.	1	Fuji Kōgyō and four other companies from the Nakajima Aircraft group merge to form Fuji Heavy Industries (FHI).
May	20	Cabinet approves procurement of enriched uranium from the US.
	31	Japan and US sign agreement on purchase of surplus US farm goods.
July	13	MITI announces five-year plan to promote the petrochemical industry.
	20	Economic Planning Agency established.
	25	Japan Housing Corporation established.
	29	Automobile liability insurance made mandatory.
Aug.	7	Sony markets world's first transistor radio.
	10	Law on temporary measures to rationalize the coal mining industry
Sept.	10	Japan joins General Agreement on Tariffs and Trade (GATT).
Oct.	13	Socialist parties merge.
Nov.	14	Japan-US Agreement for Cooperation Concerning Civil Uses of Atomic Energy signed.
	15	Liberal Party and Democratic Party merge to form Liberal Democratic Party (LDP).
	—	Riken Kōgaku Kōgyō (Ricoh) starts mass production of its Ricopy 101 copier.
Dec.	19	Atomic Energy Basic Act; Act for Establishment of the Japan Atomic Energy Commission and the Nuclear Safety Commission
Of note		Sunagawa dispute; conflict over Kita-Fuji training grounds; *Shiun-maru* case; toxic Morinaga powdered milk; electric rice cookers go on sale; increasing use of electricity by households; economic white paper outlines the road ahead.
1956		Hungarian Revolution
Feb.	19	Inaugural issue of *Shūkan Shinchō*, the first weekly magazine put out by a publishing company and the first of many weekly magazines.
Mar.	19	Japan Housing Corporation advertises for first tenants (with people moving into the Chiba Inage complex starting May 1).
Apr.	16	Japan Highway Public Corporation established.
	21	Neurological abnormalities (later recognized as Minamata disease) observed at company hospital in Minamata.
	26	Metropolitan Area Readjustment Act
May	4	Government promulgates three core laws governing nuclear power in Japan and establishes Atomic Energy Research Institute and Nuclear Fuel Development Corporation.
	9	Japan signs agreements with the Philippines on reparations and yen loans for economic development.
	14	Japan-USSR fisheries agreement signed.
	19	Science and Technology Agency established.
June	15	Act on Temporary Measures for the Promotion of the Machinery Industry
Oct.	19	Joint declaration issued on the restoration of diplomatic relations between Japan and the USSR.
Nov.	19	Yonehara—Kyoto section of Tōkaidō rail line electrified, completing electrification of entire line.

Dec.	18	United Nations General Assembly approves Japan's application for membership.
Of note		Prostitution outlawed; ♪ "Wakai o-mawari-san"; Taiyō-zoku; Stalin criticized in USSR; Poznan protests in Poland; Suez Crisis; economic white paper discusses growth and modernization (coining the "our postwar is over" phrase).
1957		**Sputnik launched**
Jan.	22	Teikoku Jinzō-kenshi (Teijin) and Tōyō Rayon (Toray) license Tetoron production technology from ICI of the UK.
Feb.	25	First Kishi cabinet takes office (announcing plans on May 3 to eradicate the three evils of corruption, violence, and poverty).
Apr.	1	First National Institutes of Technology school opens.
	16	National Development Longitudinal Expressway Construction Act
June	9	Water released from Ogouchi Dam (servicing greater Tokyo) for first time.
Aug.	27	Research reactor at Tōkai-mura, Ibaraki, goes critical.
Sept.	23	Daiei opens first store in Osaka, targeting housewives.
Nov.	5	Ministry of Education announces plans to encourage more students to go into science and technology fields.
Dec.	11	First 100 yen coins issued.
	28	NHK and Nippon Television start testing color television broadcasts.
	—	Work begins on garbage-landfilling an area of Tokyo Bay to be called Yumenoshima.
Of note		Girard case; Sunagawa case; ♪ "Yūrakuchō de aimashō"; ♪ "Que sera sera"; Jinmu Boom draws to close, followed by "nabezoko recession" (in June); (economic white paper says growth was too fast and explains why).
1958		
Jan.	—	First flight of FHI-built T1 jet trainer plane.
Feb.	5	Arabian Oil Company established.
	26	Sino-Japanese steel agreement signed.
Mar.	3	FHI produces a small "kei" passenger car (Subaru 360).
	9	Kanmon Tunnel (between Shimonoseki and Kita-Kyūshū) opened to traffic.
	31	Act on Emergency Measures Concerning Road Construction and Improvement
July	23	MITI finalizes plan to grow domestic demand by expanding plant investment in basic industries.
	25	Japan External Trade Organization (JETRO) established.
Aug.	25	Nissin Foods launches first instant ramen: Chikin Rāmen.
Oct.	8	Government submits bill to amend Police Duties Execution Act to Diet (deliberation halted Nov. 22 amid fierce opposition).
Nov.	1	Kodama express service starts on Tōkaidō rail line (cutting Tokyo–Osaka travel time to 6 hours and 50 minutes).
	27	Shōda Michiko agrees to wed Crown Prince Akihito (sparking a "Michi" Boom).
Dec.	1	New 10,000 yen bill issued.
	23	Tokyo Tower completed.
	27	Amended National Health Insurance Act
Of note		*Nankai-maru* sinks; coalminers' strike; Mt. Aso erupts; disputes over work assessments; Kanogawa typhoon; rockabilly craze; *Gekkō Kamen* takes country by storm; paid-up television subscribers top one million; start of Iwato boom (in July); economic white paper says economy is back in growth cycle.

1959		Cuban Revolution
Feb.	17	Japanese government issues first postwar foreign-currency-denominated bonds, in US.
Mar.	28	Socialist Party, Sōhyō, and others form coalition to block Japan-US Security Treaty revision and extension.
	—	Mitsubishi Petrochemical completes first stage of construction at its Yokkaichi complex.
	—	Strikes at Mitsui Miike coal mine and elsewhere protest rationalization plans.
Apr.	10	Shōda Michiko weds Crown Prince Akihito, becoming Crown Princess Michiko; wedding parade televised to eager audiences.
	14	Act on the Metropolitan Expressway Public Corporation
	15	Minimum Wage Act
	16	National Pension Act
May	26	International Olympic Committee designates Tokyo to host 1964 Olympic Games.
July	22	Kumamoto University researchers state that Minamata disease is caused by methylmercury in Japan Nitrogenous Fertilizer Company waste runoff.
Aug.	1	Nissan launches its Bluebird line, starting boom in private automobile ownership.
Sept.	1	Japan's largest blast furnace (1,500 tons) goes into operation at Yawata Iron and Steel's Tobata Works.
	11	Ministry of Finance liberalizes yen-dollar convertibility.
Nov.	2	Fishermen protesting Minamata disease clash with police at Japan Nitrogenous Fertilizer.
	11	Government liberalizes trade in 180 products.
Dec.	11	Layoffs at Mitsui's Miike mine provoke Miike labor dispute.
Of note		Ise Bay typhoon; *kaminari-zoku* motorcycle gangs; Kojima Akiko named Miss Universe; ♪ "Kuroi hanabira"; economic white paper discusses the quick economic recovery and issues for the future.
1960		Anpo and Miike disputes
Jan.	12	Ministerial conference on promoting currency exchange liberalization for trade agrees on basic policy of seeking liberalization within three years.
	19	Revised US-Japan Security Treaty and administrative agreement signed.
	25	Miike coal mine announces lockout, miners go on open-ended strike.
Feb.	8	Travel-related currency restrictions relaxed and remittances liberalized.
Mar.	31	Pneumoconiosis Act
May	19	Diet in disarray over LDP's railroaded ratification of the revised US-Japan Security Treaty.
June	1	Government promulgates amendments to Foreign Exchange Control Order, liberalizing capital transactions.
	15	Demonstrators protesting the Security Treaty's revision and extension break into Diet grounds; one woman (student Kanba Michiko) dies in the melee.
	25	Road Traffic Act
July	19	First Ikeda cabinet takes office.
	19	Central Labor Relations Commission mediates Miike dispute (miners' union accepts settlement offer on Sept. 6).
	25	Law on construction of Tōkaidō national highway

Aug.	—	Daiwa House begins trial production of prefabricated houses.
Sept.	1	Coal Mining Industry Rationalization Corporation established.
	5	LDP trumpets new policies to promote rapid growth and income doubling.
	10	NHK, Nippon Television, and other broadcasters move to color for main programming.
Nov.	1	Economic Council submits report calling for doubling national income (with 7.9% growth per year).
	1	Miike dispute resolved.
	12	Mitsui Chemicals and Mitsubishi Petrochemical receive approval to license polypropylene technology from Italian firm.
Dec.	8	Prime Minister Ikeda forms second cabinet (which approves National Income Doubling Plan on Dec. 27).
Of note		Labor unrest at Ōji Paper; tsunami from Chilean earthquake; Hagerty's car (and ultimately Eisenhower's visit) blocked; Socialist Party Chair Asanuma assassinated; Tokyo daytime population tops 10 million and Tokyo telephone exchange numbers move to triple digits; refrigerators popularized as one of the three must-haves; ♪ "Itakogasa"; ♪ "Arigataya-bushi"; economic white paper discusses Japan's economic strengths and competitiveness (explaining how investment begets investment).
1961		
Jan.	24	Canon starts marketing the Canonet, sparking the spread of EE cameras.
Apr.	1	Start of National Pension system and National Health Insurance system.
	12	Soviet Union achieves first manned space flight with Col. Yuri Gagarin aboard *Vostok 1*.
June	12	Agricultural Basic Act
	12	Honda teams win Isle of Man motorcycle races in both the 125 cc and 250 cc classes.
July	1	Installment Sales Act
Sept.	30	Water gates opened upon completion of work on Aichi Canal (Miboro Dam completed on Oct. 24).
Nov.	2	First meeting of Joint Japan-US Committee on Trade and Economic Affairs held in Hakone.
	13	Act on Advancement of Water Resources Development; Water Resources Development Public Corporation Act; Act on Temporary Measures for the Promotion of Distressed Coal Areas
	14	Construction of major industrial complexes in Tokuyama (Idemitsu Kōsan) and Mizushima (Mitsubishi Chemical) approved.
Of note		Protests over Niijima target range; Shimanaka incident; Kamikiyo coal mine fire; Muroto typhoon; abortive rightist coup attempt; ♪ "Ue o muite arukō"; ♪ "Sūdara-bushi"; number of people working in primary sector falls below 30%; "Anne" sanitary napkins go on sale; Iwato Boom draws to close in December; economic white paper discusses issues inherent in economic growth.

1962		Cuban Missile Crisis
Feb.	1	Tokyo residential population estimated to top 10 million, making Tokyo the world's first city with a population of 10 million or more.
	2	Japan signs agreement with US for reciprocal tariff cuts.
	27	NEC unveils the NEAC-2206, Japan's first domestic mainframe computer.
Mar.	1	Number of people paying NHK television subscriber fees tops 10 million.
	29	Act on Hanshin Expressway Public Corporation
Apr.	4	Act on Building Unit Ownership
May	10	Law on establishment of new industrial cities
	11	Petroleum Industry Act; Coal Mining Industry Study Group established (submits recommendations on Oct. 13).
June	2	Law to regulate particulate matter in soot and smoke emissions
Aug.	16	Regional Industrial Development Council designates 71 areas as industrial development hubs.
Sept.	12	Japan Atomic Energy Research Institute runs criticality test on first Japan-built reactor (JRR-3).
	29	Fuji-Xerox completes development of Japan's first plain-paper copier.
Oct.	1	Trade liberalized for 230 items (bringing share liberalized to 88%).
	5	Cabinet approves Comprehensive National Development Plan.
Nov.	9	Japan and China sign Liao-Takasaki Agreement.
Dec.	18	Nihon Aircraft Manufacturing unveils its YS-11 made-in-Japan passenger aircraft.
Of note		Seamen's Union strike; Mikawashima Station accident; Eniwa incident; Horie Ken'ichi crosses the Pacific solo; smog in Tokyo; thalidomide cases in West Germany; urban housing shortage boils over; twist dance craze; ♪ "Ōshō"; ♪ "Kawaii Baby"; Okutadami Dam completed; Hokuriku Tunnel opened to traffic on the Hokuriku rail line; Wakato Ōhashi bridge completed; economic white paper on the changing mechanisms of growth (and Japan at a turning point).
1963		
Feb.	10	Five municipalities amalgamated to create Kita-Kyūshū.
Apr.	25	Japan's first pedestrian overpass opens in front of Osaka Station.
June	5	Work completed on Kansai Electric Power's #4 Kurobe generating station (at Kurobe Dam).
July	11	New Housing and Urban Development Act; Act on Social Welfare for the Elderly
	12	Government designates 13 cities as New Industrial Cities and 6 locations as Special Areas for Industrial Consolidation.
	15	Amagasaki-Ritto section of Meishin Expressway opens to traffic.
	16	Amendments to the Building Standards Act (easing height restrictions)
	18	US President Kennedy issues special message on balance of payments (and Tokyo equity markets decline sharply).
Sept.	9	Price Issues Council, an Economic Planning Agency advisory organ, holds first meeting.
	14	Shin-Mitsubishi Heavy Industries successfully test-flies its MU-2 aircraft.
Oct.	26	Japan Atomic Energy Agency research group at Tōkai-mura achieves success generating electricity with atomic energy.

Nov.	1	New 1,000 yen bills issued (featuring Itō Hirobumi).
	23	First live television broadcast by satellite relay between Japan and the US (reports Kennedy assassination).
	29	MITI Industrial Structure Council submits report calling for government-business cooperation to enhance Japan's international competitiveness.
Of note		Hokuriku region snowed in; Yoshinobu kidnapping; Sayama incident; Tsurumi train derailing; Miike Mikawa mine accident; thermal-powered electricity generation exceeds hydropower generation; over 40% of farmers also hold nonfarm jobs; ♪ "Konnichiwa akachan"; economic white paper lays out path to becoming a leading industrial power.
1964		**Tokyo Olympics**
Feb.	29	Japan Railways Construction Public Corporation Act
Apr.	1	Japan gains Article 8 status in International Monetary Fund (yen becomes convertible) and liberalizes overseas travel.
	28	Japan joins the OECD.
May	16	International Metalworkers Federation–Japan Council established.
June	1	Mitsubishi Heavy Industries formed with the merger of Shin-Mitsubishi Heavy Industries, Mitsubishi Nippon Heavy Industries, and Mitsubishi Shipbuilding & Engineering.
	19	Underwater communications cable between Japan and US goes into service.
July	3	Act for the Promotion of Improvements in Special Areas for Industrial Consolidation
July	9	Residential housing site landscaping industry law
	25	Electrification of JNR San'yō Line completed.
Aug.	6	Serious water shortage in Tokyo, usage restricted to nine hours per day.
Sept.	17	Tokyo monorail begins service connecting Haneda airport and downtown Tokyo.
	29	Provisional Commission for Administrative Reform issues 16-point recommendations.
Oct.	1	Tōkaidō Shinkansen "bullet train" service initiated (four hours from Tokyo to Shin-Osaka).
	10	Tokyo Olympics open (close on Oct. 24).
	25	Prime Minister Ikeda resigns.
Nov.	9	Satō Eisaku forms first cabinet.
	12	US nuclear-powered submarine USS *Seadragon* docks in Sasebo.
Dec.	—	Japan Special Steel and Sunwave Corporation file for bankruptcy.
Of note		Reischauer stabbing; explosions at Shōwa Denkō's Kawasaki complex; Niigata earthquake; economic white paper discusses the Japanese economy and liberalization.
1965		**US starts bombing North Vietnam**
Jan.	22	Cabinet approves medium-term economic plan designed to rectify distortions introduced by income doubling (canceled in Jan. 1966).
Feb.	14	Telephone system upgraded to enable direct connections between Tokyo's 23 wards and other prefectural capitals.
Mar.	6	San'yō Special Steel declares bankruptcy with 4.8 billion yen debt overhang, making it postwar Japan's biggest bankruptcy.

May	28	Finance Minister Tanaka Kakuei announces Bank of Japan special financing for Yamaichi Securities.
June	1	Environmental Pollution Control Service Corporation Act
	2	New Tokyo International Airport Authority Act
	12	Niigata University Professor Ueki Kōmei and others reveal incidents of methylmercury poisoning in Agano River watershed.
July	1	Meishin Expressway completed with the opening of the Nagano-Nishinomiya stretch.
Nov.	10	Japan Atomic Power Company's Tōkai Power Station becomes first to generate commercial power.
	19	Cabinet approves first postwar deficit bond issue (259 billion yen).
Of note	Corruption rocks Tokyo Metropolitan Assembly; accident at Hokkaido Colliery & Steamship's Yūbari mine; demonstrations by Beheiren protesting America's war on Vietnam; massive fly infestation at Yumenoshima garbage landfill; start of Izanagi Boom (in November); economic white paper outlines the issues of stable growth.	
1966	**Cultural Revolution in China**	
Jan.	21	Japan-USSR Civil Aviation Agreement signed.
Apr.	1	Law on emergency measures for traffic safety facilities improvement program
	26	Biggest strike by Federation of Public Corporation and Government Enterprise Workers' Unions and Transport Workers' Unions since end of war.
	26	International Olympic Committee designates Sapporo to host the 1972 Winter Olympics.
June	25	Amendments to the Act on National Holidays (adding National Foundation Day, Respect for the Aged Day, and Sports Day)
July	4	Cabinet approves decision to locate New Tokyo International Airport in Sanrizuka area of Narita, Chiba.
Aug.	1	Merger of Nissan Motor and Prince Motors (kicking off regrouping of Japanese automobile industry).
Oct.	15	Toyota and Hino Motors enter into operational cooperation agreement.
	21	54 unions affiliated with Sōhyō strike in opposition to US war with Vietnam.
Nov.	24	Asian Development Bank established.
Of note	ANA plane lands in bay off Haneda Airport; Canadian Pacific plane crashes on landing at Haneda; BOAC crash near Mt. Fuji; Beatles perform in Japan, sparking boom in electric guitars sales; Tokyo declares war on traffic accidents; economic white paper looks at the path to sustainable growth.	
1967		
Mar.	13	Cabinet approves economic and social development program.
Apr.	5	Runoff from Mitsui Mining and Smelting's Kamioka Works identified as the cause of Itai-itai disease.
	15	Minobe Ryōkichi wins election as Tokyo governor with backing from Socialist and Communist parties.
	21	Prime Minister Satō sets forth the three principles restricting weapons exports.

June	6	Cabinet approves basic policy regarding liberalization of capital transactions (with relevant legislation going into effect on July 1).
	10	Tokyo University of Education Board of Regents decides to move to Tsukuba Science City.
	12	Niigata Minamata disease patients file suit against Shōwa Denkō seeking compensation.
	30	Final protocol signed in Kennedy Round for across-the-board tariff cuts.
July	20	Power Reactor and Nuclear Fuel Development Corporation established.
Aug.	1	Fuji Iron & Steel and Tōkai Steel merge.
	3	Basic Act for Environmental Pollution Control
Sept.	1	Yokkaichi asthma patients file suit seeking compensation from six local petrochemical companies.
	28	Shin-Shimizu Tunnel opens to traffic, marking the completion of the all-electric JNR Jōetsu Line.
Dec.	9	Tokyo Metropolitan Bureau of Transportation eliminates Ginza streetcar line and seven other streetcar lines.
Of note		Kyōwa Seitō lobbying scandal; US military tank cars crash and burn at Shinjuku Station; Uetsu flooding; automobile ownership tops 10 million; paid-up television subscribers top 20 million; miniskirts everywhere; go-go dance clubs popular; ♪ "Blue Chateau"; economic white paper argues for enhanced productivity and welfare.
1968		**Soviet troops invade Czechoslovakia**
Jan.	19	US nuclear-powered aircraft carrier USS *Enterprise* docks in Sasebo.
	26	Joint Japan-US Committee on Trade and Economic Affairs meets in Hawaii and agrees on defending the dollar.
Apr.	12	Kasumigaseki Building, Japan's first skyscraper, completed.
May	—	Atsugi Nylon puts pantyhose on market; Ōtsuka Foods launches "Bon Curry."
June	10	Air Pollution Control Act; Noise Regulation Act
	16	City Planning Act
July	1	Japan institutes postal code system and traffic violation ticketing system.
Sept.	26	Ministry of Health and Welfare recognizes Kumamoto Minamata disease and Niigata Minamata disease as pollution-caused diseases.
Oct.	23	Ceremonies held to commemorate the centennial of the Meiji Restoration.
Of note		University of Tokyo campus student unrest; Kin Kirō incident; Tokachi earthquake; Nittsū (Nippon Express) corruption case; Hidagawa bus accident; trouble at Shinjuku Station on International Antiwar Day; series of shooting incidents; 300 million yen heist in Fuchū; USS *Pueblo* incident; My Lai; Robert Kennedy assassinated; big-ticket company mergers (e.g., to form Mitsui Tōatsu Kagaku, Nisshō Iwai, and Kawasaki Heavy Industries); Japan's GNP second-largest in world; ♪ "Koi no kisetu"; ♪ "Hoshikage no Waltz"; economic white paper focuses on the Japanese economy in the midst of internationalization.
1969		**Apollo 11 moon landing**
Mar.	6	Yawata Iron & Steel and Fuji Iron & Steel sign merger agreement (emerging on Mar. 31, 1970, as Nippon Steel Corporation).
	—	Metropolitan Police Department declares state of emergency in war on traffic accidents.

May.	12	US secretary of commerce calls for Japan to self-restrain textile exports to the US.
	23	First pollution white paper issued.
	26	Tōmei Expressway opens full-length and links with Meishin Expressway.
	27	New Comprehensive National Development Plan approved.
June	3	Urban Renewal Act
	12	Japan's first nuclear-powered ship, *Mutsu*, launched.
	14	Minamata disease patients file suit against Chisso seeking compensation.
	23	Public Notice of Land Prices Act; Act to Establish the National Space Development Agency of Japan
July	2	Tokyo Metropolitan Government promulgates ordinance on preventing pollution.
Sept.	2	Price Stabilization Policy Council plenary session meets and agrees that curbing inflation is more important than promoting economic growth.
	29	Agricultural Policy Council issues overall agriculture policy recommendation including *gentan* (paying farmers to idle rice paddies) and other prescriptions.
Oct.	1	Unitika is established (by merger of Nichibō and Nippon Rayon).
	29	Sony and Matsushita market incompatible videotape recording systems.
Nov.	21	Satō-Nixon Joint Statement issued (including decision to return Okinawa in 1972 and to respect Japan's non-nuclear policies).
Of note		Students occupy Yasuda Auditorium building at University of Tokyo; antiwar demonstrations on Okinawa Day; folk song festivals in Shinjuku Station west concourse lead to clash with police; economic white paper examines the quest for affluence.
1970		
Feb.	3	Japan signs the Nuclear Non-Proliferation Treaty.
	11	University of Tokyo Institute of Space and Aeronautical Science launches Ohsumi, Japan's first satellite.
	16	JNR submits 10-year plan for financial restructuring with productivity improvements.
Mar.	14	Japan World Exhibition (Osaka Expo) opens in Osaka (runs to Sept. 13).
Apr.	19	Sino-Japanese memorandum trade agreement signed.
	24	Law on emergency measures for critically underpopulated areas
May	7	Government promulgates special measures granting Okinawa citizens suffrage pre-reversion (to include the Nov. 15 election).
	18	Nationwide Shinkansen Railways Construction and Improvement Act; Act on Punishment of Unlawful Seizure of Aircraft
	20	Honshū-Shikoku Bridge Authority Establishment Act
June	1	Act on the Settlement of Environmental Pollution Disputes (Headquarters for Environmental Pollution Countermeasures established July 31)
	23	1960 US-Japan Security Treaty automatically extended.
July	18	First photochemical smog alert issued, in Suginami, Tokyo.
Aug.	2	Tokyo's Ginza, Shinjuku, Ikebukuro, and Asakusa areas close main roads to vehicular traffic to create pedestrian malls on Sundays and holidays.
	11	Cabinet decides on emergency measures to deal with sludge pollution in Tagonoura, Shizuoka Prefecture.

Nov.	3	US Department of the Treasury issues finding of dumping against Japanese television sets.
Dec.	25	Government promulgates 14 laws relating to pollution, including Act to Punish Environmental Crimes and Water Pollution Prevention Act
Of note		*Yodo* hijacking; gas explosion at Osaka subway construction site; Mishima Yukio commits suicide; Izanagi Boom draws to close (in July); economic white paper is on the economy's new dimensions.
1971		**Currency turmoil**
Jan.	13	Railway Construction Council recommends building the Tōhoku, Jōetsu, and Narita Shinkansen lines.
	20	Work completed on the Kashima Petrochemical Complex in Ibaraki Prefecture.
Feb.	22	Riot police clash with demonstrators protesting the expropriation of land for the new international airport in Narita.
Mar.	8	Japan Textile Federation announces it will voluntarily curtail exports to the US.
	25	Dai-ichi Bank and Nippon Kangyō Bank sign merger agreement (to take effect with the creation of the Dai-ichi Kangyō Bank on Oct. 1).
	26	First residents move into Tama New Town housing development.
	26	Tokyo Electric Power's Fukushima nuclear power plant goes into operation.
May	12	Mitsubishi Motors signs contract providing for capital infusion from Chrysler.
June	1	Workers' Property Accumulation Promotion Act
	5	Keio Plaza Hotel opens as first high-rise in West Shinjuku area.
	17	Okinawa Reversion Agreement signed.
July	1	Environment Agency established.
	15	US President Nixon announces he will visit China (first Nixon shock).
Aug.	15	US announces it is suspending the dollar's convertibility to gold (second Nixon shock).
	28	Japan provisionally moves to floating exchange rates.
Sept.	14	Central Conference for Environmental Pollution Control Measures established (submits report on airport noise on Dec. 27).
	28	Tokyo Governor Minobe declares war on garbage.
Oct.	15	Settlement reached in Japan-US textile negotiations (bilateral agreement signed on Jan. 3, 1972).
	25	United Nations General Assembly approves Chinese (PRC) membership and expels Taiwan (ROC).
Dec.	19	Yen is appreciated to new base rate of 308 yen to the dollar.
Of note		Narita Airport opening delayed by strife; Okinawa struggle; Ponzi schemes; *Bandai* crash near Hakodate; plane collision over Shizukuishi; Kawasaki landslide experiment goes wrong; Matsumotorō restaurant in Hibiya Park burns down; explosive device disguised as Christmas tree blows up in Shinjuku; ♪ "Shiretoko ryojō"; ♪ "Watashi no jōkamachi"; emperor travels to Europe; NHK General TV goes all-color; McDonald's opens in Japan; Nissin Foods starts sale of Cup Noodles; economic white paper is about achieving balance between domestic and overseas demand.
1972		**Normalization of Sino-Japanese relations**
Feb.	3	Winter Olympics open in Sapporo (close on Feb. 13).
Mar.	15	San'yō Shinkansen goes into service between Osaka and Okayama.

May	15	Japan regains administrative authority over Okinawa.
	26	First environmental white paper issued.
June	11	Minister of International Trade and Industry Tanaka Kakuei publishes his *Building a New Japan*.
	16	Industrial Relocation Promotion Law
	22	Nature Conservation Act; amendments to the Air Pollution Control Act and the Water Pollution Prevention Act
	23	Amendments to the Act on Social Welfare for the Elderly (making medical care free for people 70 or older)
	23	UK floats pound sterling (this "pound shock" causes Japanese stocks to fall sharply the following day).
July	7	Prime Minister Tanaka Kakuei forms first cabinet.
	24	Tsu District Court finds collective illegal behavior by the defendant firms in the Yokkaichi pollution suit (verdict is final).
Aug.	7	Panel to discuss Tanaka's *Building a New Japan* issues first report.
Sept.	6	Tokyo, Kanagawa, and Chiba prefectures declare Tokyo Bay a dead sea.
Oct.	3	Central Conference for Environmental Pollution Control Measures recommends restrictions on automobile exhaust emissions.
Nov.	24	Restrictions on how much money outbound Japanese travelers may take with them are relaxed.
Dec.	21	High levels of PCB detected in inland sea fish.
Of note		Red Army holes up in Asama lodge; building fire in Sennichimae (Osaka); Lod Airport massacre; JAL crash in New Delhi; JAL crash in Moscow; fire in Hokuriku Tunnel; Casio markets Casio Mini calculator; panda boom; economic white paper focuses on building a new welfare state.
1973		**Vietnam War ends**
Jan.	25	Cabinet adopts Land Policy Outline (including new property taxes and notification requirement for large-scale transactions).
Feb.	12	Dollar devalued 10% (yen appreciated Feb. 14 and exchange rate floated).
Mar.	5	Kōbe Bank and Taiyō Bank agree to merge and become Taiyō Kōbe Bank as of Oct. 1.
June	11	Tokyo study finds Tokyo Bay fish and shellfish contaminated with PCB.
July	6	Act on Emergency Measures against Acts of Buying Up or Holding Back Sales of Goods Related to Everyday Life
	25	Agency for Natural Resources and Energy established.
Oct.	5	Act on Compensation for Pollution-Related Health Damage
	6	Fourth Arab-Israeli War (Yom Kippur War) breaks out.
	17	Organization of Arab Petroleum Exporting Countries (OAPEC) resolves to cut back oil exports to countries supporting Israel.
	23	Exxon and Shell raise crude oil prices 30% (an "oil shock" for Japan).
Nov.	2	People start hoard-buying toilet paper, detergents, and other household products.
	9	Federation of Electric Power Companies calls for 10% cut in power consumption (including shutting off neon lights and other conservation measures).
	16	Cabinet approves outline of emergency measures for petroleum industry and establishes petroleum policy promotion headquarters within the cabinet.

Dec.	22	Petroleum Supply and Demand Adjustment Act; Act on Emergency Measures for Stabilizing Living Conditions
Of note		Ageo Station occupied by protesters; JAL plane hijacked in Dubai; Kim Dae-jung abducted from Tokyo hotel room; Taiyō Department Store fire in Kumamoto; Suginami (Tokyo) mounts major campaign to get garbage situation under control; rampant inflation; ♪ "Kandagawa"; ♪ "Gakuseigai no kissaten"; economic white paper explores welfare in the absence of inflation.
1974		
Feb.	1	Medical fees raised 19% (and another 16% on Oct. 1).
	5	Fair Trade Commission orders Petroleum Association and 12 wholesalers to rescind their agreements on production sharing and price setting.
	25	House of Representatives Budget Committee holds intensive hearings on prices (designed to ferret out malicious sales practices, window-of-opportunity price hikes, and the like).
Apr.	20	Japan-China Air Transport Agreement signed.
June	1	Electrical power charges raised 74% for industrial customers, 29% for households.
	25	National Land Use Planning Act (National Land Agency established the next day)
Oct.	1	Tsunami of price hikes for items including rice, travel, and postage.
	3	MITI announces gist of five-year plan to increase petroleum reserves.
Dec.	9	Prime Minister Miki names first cabinet.
	17	Ministerial Meeting on Economic Measures confirms plans for slower growth.
Of note		Korean President Park Chung-hee assassinated; explosions rock major companies; crude oil leakage at Mizushima; Onoda Hirō surrenders and returns to Japan; Watergate scandal in US; Tokyo population shrinks for first time since end of war; national average residential land prices slip for first time since end of war; real economic growth rate is minus 1.4% (first annual decline since end of war); economic white paper looks beyond economic growth.

Index

exchange rates, 9, 133
See also currency value
exports. *See* imports and exports

F

family
  ie system, 15, 21
  social structure in farm families, 18–22, 76, 96
  See also children
farming employment
  health and, 140, 142
  income, 1960, 43
  income, 1970, 95–96
  income, pre-rapid growth era, 17, 21–22, 107
  rates, 1950, 9, 18–19
  See also employment
farming employment, labor outflow during
  great migration, 76, 77, 78, 84–85, 90, 92, 102
  full- to part-time employment shift, 95–96
  industrialization and, 148, 149
  mortality rates lowered, 140
  See also great migration
farming households
  automobile ownership, 50
  budgets of, 23
  family social structure, 18–22, 76, 96
  See also rural villages
farming process
  population density and, 93
  pre-rapid growth era, 21
  production curtailments, 96
farm villages. *See* rural villages
fashion industry, 52
fathers, social status in rural villages, 19, 20, 21
financial sector, zaibatsu dissolution, 15, 16, 148
Fogel, Robert W., 139
food and diet, 40
  consumer revolution changes, 49–50
  dining habits, 46–47, 48, 50
  for employees, during great migration, 79–80
    in farm households, pre-rapid growth era, 22, 24
    government rationing, pre-rapid growth era, 24
    "instant" foods advent, 49
    supermarkets, 72–73
    See also health
Four Dragons, 158
France, 53, 155–156
Fujin Kōron (magazine), 32
Fuji Steel, 60
Fujiyama Aiichirō, 118
Fukutake Tadashi, 18

G

Gakusei kekkon (Student Newlyweds, Kimura), 13, 25
GDP. *See* gross national product (GNP)
"Gendai Nihon no kaika" (The Civilization of Modern-Day Japan, Natsume), 159–160
Gendai seiji: 1955 igo (Contemporary Politics Since 1955, Masumi), 118
gender
  employee turnover and, 81
  of great migration migrants, 77, 79
  life expectancy and, 9, 10, 136–137, 139–140
  See also men; women
"Genjō to sono haikei kara mita 21-seiki no iryō seido" (Negishi and Naitō), 143
Germany, 60
  West Germany, 53, 88–89, 125
GNP. *See* gross national product (GNP)
Gone with the Wind (film), 29
Gotō Yonosuke ("Mr. White Paper"), 56–57
Great Britain, 59–60, 138–139
great migration, 76–96
  employment conditions during, 79–80
  end of rapid-growth era and, 105–106
  households numbers, 91–92, 99, 101–102, 103
  labor market changes during, 84–90
  manufacturing sector changes during, 86–90, 98–100
  migrants' demographics, 77–83

political support and, 130–131
population density issues, 92–96
population statistics, 76–77, 85, 91–96
wage disparity during, 84–86, 127–128
See also employment, during great
migration; farming employment, labor
outflow during great migration
gross domestic product (GDP), term use, 155
Gross National Happiness (GNH) index,
157
gross national product (GNP)
agriculture percentage, 95
alternatives to, 157
China, 53, 54
definition and limitations, 154–157
growth rates, 107
income-doubling plan and, 128
in 1946, 14, 111
during oil crises, 105
growth metrics. *See* economic indicators
growth rates
in 1970s, 103
in 1988, 154
in 1990s, 154
GNP and, 107
Iwato Boom, 51, 115
Izanagi Boom, 50–53, 60, 87
during oil crises, 104

H

Hachikō square (Shibuya), 24, 26–27
happiness, 155–156, 157
Hatoyama Ichirō, 119
health
health insurance system establishment,
during rapid-growth era, 142–145
infant mortality rates, 140–142, 145, 151
medical modernization, 139–140, 141
Minamata disease, 146
pollution's effects on, 143–151
WWII effects on, 14–15, 17, 139–140
See also food and diet; life expectancy;
positive effects of rapid growth era
Health Insurance Act (1922), 142
Heibon Punch (magazine), 52

high mass consumption society, 157–158
See also consumer revolution
historical period classifications, 10
home birth, 29
Honda, 58
Honda Tatsuo, 18
Hosokawa Hajime, 146–147
hotels, 45–46
households
consumer durables in, during great
migration, 92
end of rapid-growth era and, 105
increased number, during great migration,
91–92, 99, 101–102, 103
rural-urban comparisons, 25, 28, 41, 91–92
See also consumer revolution
household savings rate, 107–109
housing
danchi (public apartment complexes),
46–47
infrastructure projects, 25, 46–47, 142
interior changes, 50
materials and construction, health and, 142
rural villages, pre-rapid growth era, 19–21
urban areas, changes in, 46–48
urban areas, pre-rapid growth era, 24,
25–29
hunger, 14

I

Ibuka Masaru, 110
Ichimada Hisato, 58
ie system, 15, 21
Ikeda Hayato, 96, 113
election, 1960, 118, 128
income-doubling plan, 123–129
imports and exports
balance of payment ceiling and, 109, 123
import of technology, 99, 101, 106–107
investment and, 108–109, 134
oil, 105
postwar importance of, 109–112
prewar importance of, 102, 109
raw materials, 14, 56, 61, 111–112
steel production and, 14, 61, 100

social structure, pre-rapid growth era, 22–32
See also great migration; rural-urban comparisons; rural villages; Tokyo
urban areas, pre-rapid growth era, 17, 22–32
art and culture, 22, 29–31
housing, 24, 25–29
illumination, 31–32
rural villages, compared, 24, 25, 43
transportation infrastructure, 24, 31
urban employment. *See* employment
urban infrastructure
consumer revolution changes in, 43–50
hotels, 45–46
housing, 25, 46–48, 142
infant mortality rates and, 141
investment in, 134
Olympics-related changes, 43–45, 45–46, 47
population density and, 94
roads, 44–45
subways, 46
See also construction
Uzawa Hirofumi, 141

V

villages. *See* rural villages
voter support, 130–132
See also political context of rapid-growth era

W

wages. *See* income
washing machines, 35–37, 41–43, 50, 53
See also consumer durables, diffusion of
Watanabe Shin'ichi, 18
water utilities, 28
waterways, 44–45, 148
wealth, 155–156
See also income
West Germany, 53, 88–89, 125
wholesale price index, 112
See also consumer prices
wholesale-retail price disparity, 112–115

women
clothing and fashion, 34–35, 52
graduation rates, pre-rapid growth era, 9
life expectancy, 9, 10, 136–137, 139–140
in textile industry, 79
washing machines and, 37
See also gender
World War II, impact of
children's physique, 15, 17
life expectancy, 139–140
living standards, 14
postwar reforms, 15, 98–100
rubble used to fill waterways, 45
surrender's effect on national spirit, 14, 16
urban neighborhoods destroyed, 25

Y

Yamaichi Securities, 129
Yanagita Kunio, 40
Yawata Iron & Steel, 59, 60
Yawata Steel union, 121–122
yen, currency value. *See* exchange rates
Yokkaichi, 148
Yomiuri Giants, 38
Yomiuri Shimbun, 84, 125
Yoshida Ken'ichi, 10–11
Yoshida Shigeru, 119, 120

Z

zaibatsu (financial and industry conglomerates), 15, 16, 148

About the Author

Yoshikawa Hiroshi

Yoshikawa Hiroshi is the president of Rissho University. He was born in Tokyo in 1951, received his B.A. from the University of Tokyo Faculty of Economics and his Ph.D. from Yale University, and subsequently taught as an assistant professor at the State University of New York (Albany), an associate professor at the Institute of Social and Economic Research at Osaka University, an associate professor at the University of Tokyo, and a professor at the University of Tokyo Graduate School of Economics. Yoshikawa specializes in macroeconomics and the Japanese economy.

His publications include *Macro-Econophysics* (Cambridge University Press, 2017, with Aoyama Hideaki, Fujiwara Yoshi, Ikeda Yuichi, Iyetomi Hiroshi, and Souma Wataru); *Defurēshon* [Deflation] (Nikkei Publishing Inc., 2013); *Japan's Lost Decade*, revised and expanded edition (I-House Press, 2008); *Reconstructing Macroeconomics: A Perspective from Statistical Physics and Combinatorial Stochastic Processes* (Cambridge University Press, 2007, with Aoki Masanao); and *Macroeconomics and the Japanese Economy* (Oxford University Press, 1995).

About the Translator

Fred Uleman

Born and raised in Pittsburgh, Uleman moved to Tokyo in 1963 following graduation from the University of Michigan. He has been translating professionally since the late 1960s, primarily business and political texts and always Japanese to English.

（英文版）高度成長　日本を変えた六〇〇〇日
Ashes to Awesome: Japan's 6,000-Day Economic Miracle

2021年3月27日　第1刷発行

著　者　　吉川　洋
訳　者　　ウレマン・フレッド
発行所　　一般財団法人出版文化産業振興財団
　　　　　〒101-0051 東京都千代田区神田神保町2-2-30
　　　　　電話　03-5211-7283
　　　　　ホームページ　https://www.jpic.or.jp/

印刷・製本所　　大日本印刷株式会社